D1714873

Letters to Mikey

Messages of Hope and
Optimism for Young Americans

by

Glenn Cort

Letters to Mikey
Copyright © 2023 Glenn Cort

ISBN: 979-8-8655-5565-0
Hardcover

Dedication and Thanks

My gratitude goes out to all of the young people I've spoken with during this chapter of my life. I've seen, in your wide-open eyes, a natural grasp of the path intended for all of us, which greatly inspires me.

Likewise to my daughter Katelin and sons John and Mikey, as a humble parent and at most times just an ordinary guy, to behold your curiosity and untaught comprehension, is to witness the miracle of life itself, and drives me to be a believer.

Mr. Banker, having gotten to know you better it comes as no surprise that you were Mikey's favorite teacher. Thank you for helping me better understand the age group for which I seek to assist, and to bring this book into focus.

Finally, to the authors whom I refer to in this book, it is because of your great effort to become philosophers and to write your books that I found the passion to write mine. Thank you.

Table of Contents

Forward

Introduction

Chapter 1: Human Nature- The Good News   13

Chapter 2: Human Nature- The Not So Good News   21

Chapter 3: The Many Paths to Greatness   28

Chapter 4: The Intended Path   45

Chapter 5: The Path: Grand Finale   72

Chapter 6: The Rise of the Bucking Broncos   77

Chapter 7: Our Unraveling Basic Ingredients
     and Natural Law   91

Chapter 8: The Play by Play   111

Chapter 9: The New Normal   130

Chapter 10: Breakthrough   140

Chapter 11: Deadly Myths   150

Chapter 12: Voices of Evil and Types of Harm   164

Chapter 13: Making Change   176

Chapter 14: Race   181

Chapter 15: Final Thoughts   186

Glossary   197

Bibliography   214

Forward

The Mikey Man

Michael James Cort, otherwise known as the Mikey Man, was born on July 24, 2003, and is the youngest of my three kids. The other day was his 18th birthday, and in a few weeks, he will be going off to college and officially making me what they call an "empty nester." Ever since I can remember, I've written a letter to Mikey on his birthday. In fact, we've been exchanging letters since he was old enough to read and write. This year was a particularly important one, with him having just graduated high school and leaving home to begin the rest of his life. If I didn't get a few happy tears with my birthday card this year, the Mikey Man would surely think that Dad was off his game, and we couldn't have that... So, I dug in!

My mind searched deeply for the right thing to say, and for reasons which I couldn't fully understand at that moment, I felt incredible pressure to lift my son up at this particular time in his life. Then it happened- Hours turned into days. I couldn't stop writing to my son- one page streamed into the next, and as his birthday approached, I realized I had a major problem on my hands. How would I tell the Mikey Man that I can't give him his letter because I decided to write a book?! Then, in a single moment on his birthday, without my letter in hand, I came to him and said:

"Mikey, I love you beyond words. Of all the fatherly advice and greatest wisdom I will ever convey to you is that we are placed in this world to be a part of a greater connected community. We can't create happiness and peace for ourselves when there is so much unrest and unhappiness across our street or elsewhere in our world. None of us can change the entire world but each of us can change for the better the world we inhabit. Let us not underestimate the impact that we can make. My son, *the* secrets to your enjoyment of life, and to your generation living with harmony, free of hate, and terrible disagreement, are WAY too complex to summarize... but you know me, my man, I am going to try."

So here goes.

Introduction

Over the 54 years of my life, I've felt a few powerful impulses. I didn't know where they came from or what was behind them. They were just there, and I followed them without knowing why. Some of these impulses have put me on the brink of death, while others have propelled me to freedoms beyond my wildest dreams. The motivating force gripping me now is rooted in a single sentiment: I care about you- my young friend- deeply. More importantly, is for you to know that you are surrounded by more caring, decent, and helpful people than you may realize. In fact, there are millions of adults who have the correct sense to help guide you at this important time in your lives. However, you wouldn't necessarily know that, given how many of us "grown-ups" have been acting in the last few years.

As young people, you've had to live through Covid 19, BLM, Stop Asian Hate, Defund the Police, Critical Race Theory, #MeToo, Karen's, and Proud Boys, just to name just a few of the political issues that have ripped us apart and pitted one American against the other. You are growing up in the most confusing political climate that I've ever seen. I am a lawyer, a former Assistant District Attorney, and a father of three who has voted in every election since I was 18. In all my years, I have never felt concerned about the inability of Americans to live, work, and cooperate with one another as I do today. Our inability to get along seems to find a new peak every day. Not all of the issues are bad. In fact, some are necessary, except for Karens and Proud Boys, of course... but the time for jokes about this stuff is over. People being more angry and divided than ever before is taking a toll on your generation- many of you have told me so.

In September 2020, I was asked to teach a course on modern construction techniques to high school seniors in Boston, having spent almost thirty years in a unique field focused on making it more efficient to build schools and other buildings. I was honored, excited, and nervous. Sadly, only days into the course, Covid kicked into high gear. As our in-person classes turned into online Zoom events, it quickly became apparent that the more technology we used to stay connected, the further we grew apart.

I remember feeling sad, sensing the opportunity of making long-term relationships slipping away. I could tell that my students were down in the dumps from the effects of Covid. Most of them seemed exhausted, and it was hard for us to engage in meaningful conversations. There existed an overwhelming yet generalized sense of noise and confusion that dominated our classroom. Most of the kids wore upon their remarkable faces what I can only describe as a look of fed-upness with the world around them. What I will never forget is a few of my students shaking their weary heads left to right... and saying to me, "Mr. Cort, things are just so messed up out there." The only thing that seemed clear to me in that moment was that what they were experiencing was a whole lot more than Covid.

That spring, I spent time speaking to many of Mikey's friends at his high school graduation events, and I couldn't help but notice the same general sense of uncertainty. I began to learn that their concern was mostly with our government and how much disagreement there was about our politics. When I asked the meaning of the word 'politics' most of the responses I received were singular words such as violence, hate, and division. I don't recall anyone being proud of our country. As I ventured into Mikey's younger nephews, cousins, and their friends my worst fears were coming home to roost. Many of the young people I spoke with were questioning the goodness of the world around them for the first time and in new ways. Factually, there are more teens feeling lonely, isolated, and depressed than ever before. In fact, "between 2009 and 2019, there was a 40 percent spike in high schoolers saying that they experienced 'persistent feelings of sadness or hopelessness'" (Ritchie, 2021). But in this book, I'm not going to bore you with too many statistics when you know better than I do what you are going through. What I do know is that the alarm bell is ringing. I have taken your words as a wake-up call.

We need to cut through the noise and confusion and reestablish our sense of confidence in our country. While the America you live in today may have reached a low point, it doesn't need to be the America you wake up in tomorrow. The truth is that when it comes to our government and politics, what you have been experiencing is a total *aberration*[1]. {Please note: In an effort to make this book as enjoyable as possible to read, whenever I use a word which I believe to be particularly powerful, I will place it in *italics* and place its definition in the footer of the page. There is also a full glossary of these words in the back. I have used Siri for all definitions. I want to thank The Apple Company Inc. because I have found Siri's definitions very helpful. I hope you do too.} What you have been experiencing in the last few years should be totally unwelcome in any normal world. You and your age group need to know that voices of reason will overcome. They always have and always will!

There are many people out there like me who are sorry to see this happening. We understand the root causes of how we got here and have the tools to help your generation see things for what they truly are and for what they can be. Believe it or not, you can grow up in a country that you love and in a city or town where you feel like you belong and where you can trust your elected officials instead of making fun of them.

Political debate in this country can be *civil*[2] and even enjoyable. This is what I experienced when I practiced law at the Massachusetts Attorney General's office and as a young Assistant District Attorney in Boston during the 1990s. Good people disagreed often, but we always did so with *dignity*[3] and *respect*[4]. In my many years in business, I have worked with people of all different backgrounds and opposing opinions and have found the majority of people are committed to solving problems for the betterment of everyone. You will also find this to be true in your life. It may seem hard to believe right now, but there are many reasons for you to be optimistic about our country and your future. Exploring why this is true is what this book   is   all   about!

I have long held a theory about life and about people. It goes like this: at any given moment in America, 90% of people have the

---

1. aberration: a departure from what is normal, usual or expected, typically one that is unwelcome
2. civil: courteous and polite
3. dignity: the state or quality of being worthy of honor or respect
4. respect: due regard for the feelings, wishes, rights, or traditions of others

desire and abilities to help us achieve our societal goals. The fact is, that in real life if you got in a room with someone whom you thought you disagreed with, in most cases you would leave that room respecting and even liking the other person- even if you remained competitors. Ninety percent of people hold enough belief in common, and can communicate well enough to be helpful citizens. This means of course that about 10% of us currently lack these abilities. The 10%ers are mostly much older than you are, which presents us with an amazing opportunity. More on this later...

Of course, we all have our moments, so it may not be possible to get everyone to behave as we would like all of the time. There will always be disagreements between people. Of course we can't change that, but what if we could educate all people to share a sort of moral code when it comes to how we interact with one another? What if we could all learn to make a choice, to communicate so that we could disagree without being rude? To never talk down to each other? Wouldn't that make the world a nicer place to be? We will define this code together as a goal of the book and make every effort to achieve it. *Morality*[5] is defined as *"the principles concerning the distinction between right and wrong or good and bad behaviors."* Nothing more, nothing less. Morality is something that is taught and learned and won or lost along our journey of life.

My impulse for writing this book began out of love for my son. It was purely emotional, so I wasn't planning on doing a ton of research to support my own ideas and theories, but that changed. I found some time in selling my business (unexpectedly) and moved to an island to research my thoughts. While there, I started reading more than I had ever done before. I found myself devouring as much information as I could, ripping through dozens upon dozens of books, eager to re-open my mind to all kinds of things. I started with the old stuff, from the likes of Socrates, Aristotle, Buddha, and Cicero (I love the word Cicero so much, I may refer to all the ancient philosophers as the "Cicero's of the world.")

I must admit that at first, I found most of the books very long

---

5. morality: the principles concerning the distinction between right and wrong or good and bad behaviors

and boring with a lot of huge words that I couldn't understand. So I began to use the Siri App on my phone to define terms, and it made my search for meaning much easier. The more I read, the more I felt alive! The books amazed me. The people who wrote

them amazed me as well. I was having what they call a full-fledged *revelation*[6] or an epiphany, or both at once! The similarity of opinions spanning hundreds of years, if not thousands, from books about history, religion, and philosophy, was undeniable. There were certain themes that seemed to be recurring over and over again. These philosophies resonated with my own life experience.

I began to realize that when it comes to our knowledge about what values and morals people need to get along with one another, we humans really know our shit! And it's not just our ability to get along. It's our understanding of how happiness is achieved and maintained as well. Certain ways of thinking and acting cause us to grow character, which, as it turns out, is the single word that matters most. Our most worshiped leaders since the dawn of *civilization*[7] all share certain character traits, as well as belief systems and ways of approaching their lives. There is also vast agreement that these behaviors can be learned rather easily and maintained with practice.

So there I was in my bathrobe, on this remote island in the middle of the winter, books piled up at my side, my scruff now grown into a full beard, and my dog Gracie lying on the floor with her head turned in classic inquisitive dog fashion, looking up at me as I was jumping for joy! In a world where everyone has been questioning up from down, left from right, and good from evil, I had RE-learned in a few months in the library... what I simply set out to tell my son; that **there is- actually- right from wrong when it comes to how to behave**! However, my elation didn't last for long. It wasn't a moment after this rediscovery that I had a sinking feeling. My forehead

---

6. revelation: a surprising and previously unknown fact, especially one that is made known in a dramatic way

7. civilization: the stage of human social and cultural development and organization that is considered most advanced

tightened…(I think I saw it on Gracies face too) as I thought to myself, **If being a moral person is so well-established by experts, then why are so many people behaving so badly? <u>Why aren't all these fantastic books working?!</u>**

The answers to this question are, no doubt, complex but are not out of our reach. We can't fix our problems if we aren't honest about how we got here. We've had a few political leaders in the last few years who have underestimated the impact of their own behaviors and, as well, did not understand how the internet would change things. This combination has done a lot of damage. But we only become a part of the problem if we blame any one person. We are done following the script that got us into this mess. We don't get anywhere by putting people down. It isn't one person who got us into this mess, and it won't be one person who gets us out of it. We are all in this together.

I have come to believe that as tricky as life is, there are a few truths that we can always count on. The few that I will speak of in the pages that follow have been tried and tested, and will forever prove themselves to be true. For example, in life, to have success, there is a certain way to behave depending on the situation. There is a time to be *theatrical[8], dramatic, emotional, and unconventional[9].* In your social life, for example, with your friends, go nuts, be wild and radical, enjoy, and have fun. In fact the wilder, the better- I encourage it. But in governmental settings it just doesn't work. When leaders of organizations make it normal, to be carefree, casual, and loose with facts, they call into question truth, which is the foundation that a civilized society (or any functional organization) stands upon. When we remove truth, distrust of other people follows. Today, in America, we are arguing about obvious things, such as if Elmo is red or blue, or if the world is really flat. Reliable and reassuring standards that used to weave us together have become twisted out of shape. The media fuels the fire, and this has led to what I would call an *epidemic[10]* of misunderstanding and hate.

---

8. theatrical: exaggerated and excessively dramatic
9. unconventional: not based on or conforming to what is generally done or believed
10. epidemic: (of a disease) occurring widely in a community at a particular time

My mission is to help future generations bond together through the re-establishment of a few basic truths. Notice- I say *re*-establishment because they are rooted in things that pre-exist. Much of the truth we need to understand better, (to relearn or pay more attention to) is about our human nature- which we all share. Having a deeper understanding of how all of us think and being more mindful of it, will help us get back on track. Great American poet Robert Frost said, "Education is the ability to listen to almost anything without losing your temper or self-confidence." Education can make miracles happen. With the right education, we can ALL agree on what the truth looks like, and we can all become healers and beacons of hope, maybe even a few of us old farts...but that would only be icing on the cake!

There will always be a few people who seek to tear us apart. These are our truth deniers who make every effort to deprive us of the preservation of shared truth. Lately, they have become successful. But it is OK. We are a totally advanced society, fully capable of rejecting distortions of reality. We can and will overcome their voices. Like our weatherman on TV, who can predict when a storm is coming based on certain conditions in the atmosphere. Similarly, we know what causes people to become overly *self-righteous*[11], angry and dead set on interfering with the type of peace you want to see in the world. We do not have to let them pull us down. Instead, we are going to lift them up!

There is a reason why our government withstood the attack on our Capitol on January 6th, 2021. The 90%ers prevailed! But Government is complex. There is a reason why so many of us get bent out of shape. Author William Damon put the challenges of an organized society this way, "How should the world's resources be allocated among all the people who lay claim to them? What does it mean to deserve something? How should we balance the rights of someone who has earned something against the rights of someone who may need it more?_These are problems... on a grand scale and, despite centuries of debate, have eluded resolution. (Damon, 2008, p.31) If we blame one side or the other we grow further apart from them. We cannot turn a blind eye to people with whom we disagree. People were

---

11. self-righteous: having or characterized by a certainty, especially an unfounded one, that one is totally correct or morally superior

wrong to express their frustration with violence, climbing the walls of the Capitol building and killing a police officer. Without blaming anyone, we will explore in the pages ahead why people come to disagree so badly and what we can do to prevent anything like this from happening again.

We seem to set aside our differences in our looks, race, colors, and differing opinions in so many areas of our lives together. We seem to have success in our pop culture. Consider how (most) everyone loves the Super Bowl halftime shows as an example and in team sports. We get along regardless of our age, race, religion, or skin color, yet we continue to distrust our *politicians*[12]. If not improved, these conditions will continue to cast a dark cloud over your future. We can't have that.

Any advice book worth reading, especially one that attempts to make sense of politics, needs to have its serious moments, but I promise I will try to keep things fast-moving and fun. I set out to write a simple pep talk to my kid, and I want it to read like that. I want to place a few golden nuggets of knowledge directly on your tongue and make it easy to digest. Like the drive-through line at Chick-fil-A! One of my main goals is to make you smile, but at the same time, I ask that you really think through these impactful ideas and issues.

If many of you engage in the materials in this book, your generation can reach unbelievable heights. You are simply stronger and more capable than you think (proof of this follows). By regaining your trust in the good of the human spirit, and in our country, I believe your generation can free yourselves of terrible disagreement and hate forever! These aren't false promises. It's possible. Let's start a movement, by tapping into our greatest resource- YOU!

Now, as my oldest son John always says, "Let's GOOOHHHH!!!"

---

12. politician: a person who is professionally involved in politics, especially as a holder of or a candidate for an elected office

Chapter 1: Human Nature- The Good News

There are some things about people that are undeniable. Take this statement about a smile:

"A smile," someone once said, costs nothing but gives much. It enriches those who receive without making poorer those who give. It takes but a moment, but the memory of it sometimes lasts forever. None is so rich or mighty that he can get along without it and none is so poor that he cannot be made rich by it. Yet a smile cannot be bought, begged, or stolen, for it is something that is of no value to anyone until it is given away. Some people are too tired to give you a smile... Give them one of yours, as none needs a smile so much as he who has no more to give" (Carnegie, 2022).

Can any one of us deny the truth in these words? Do it now. Please try smiling and tell me that you don't feel a bit better? It's human nature.

As you may know, there are people who dedicate their whole lives to helping us understand how we best learn, cope, and thrive. They also grapple with that little word called happiness. The study of what makes us happy or to flourish has been around for thousands of years. The "Cicero's of the World" have established certain truths that I find to be *incontrovertible*[13] but it is the scientific discoveries of the last few years about the human brain, and what makes us tick, that will help us best achieve our goals. These findings are so important I want to provide a few definitions of the fields of study in this area:

1. Science- the intellectual and practical systematic study of the structure and behavior of the physical and natural world through observation, experimentation, and the testing of theories against the evidence obtained
2. Psychology- the scientific study of the human mind and its functions
3. Social Psychology- the branch of psychology that deals with social interactions
4. Philosophy- the study of the fundamental nature of

---

13. incontrovertible: not able to be denied or disputed

knowledge, reality, and existence, especially when considered as an academic discipline

5. Epistemology- the branch of philosophy concerned with knowledge, the investigation of what distinguishes justified belief from opinion

6. Biology- the study of living organisms divided into many specialized fields that cover their morphology, physiology, anatomy, behavior, origin, and distribution

7. Neuroscience—any and all the sciences, such as neurochemistry and experimental psychology, which deal with the structure and function of the nervous system and brain

8. Cognitive scientists- the study of thought, learning, and mental organization, which draws on aspects of psychology, linguistics, philosophy, and computer modeling

9. Sociology:-the study of the development structure and functioning of human society and social problems

10. Physiology- an expert or student in the branch of biology that deals with the normal functioning of living organisms and their parts

11. Biochemistry– the study of chemical process in living organisms such as humans

12. Anthropology– the study of human societies and cultures and their development

13. Psychiatry- the study and treatment of mental illness, emotional disturbance, and abnormal behavior; mental illness as "any disease of the mind; the psychological state of someone who has emotional or behavioral problems serious enough to require psychiatric intervention

14. Geneticist- an expert or student in heredity and the variation of inherited characteristics; someone involved with the study of human genes

It typically takes someone more than eight years to become a Doctor ("a qualified practitioner of medicine") and over twelve years to earn a PhD, the highest possible degree known to mankind. They wear white coats and use expensive equipment to test babies, toddlers, rats, mice, and monkeys, doing trials until things are proven true. They do life's most important work of separating opinion from real and justifiable fact. For example, a smile makes us feel better- I give this advice on a hunch and some of our hunches are true, but you will have more success in your life if you are a person who can back up your opinions with justifiable facts. The Ph.D. watches the "neurons" in our heads (whatever those are?) fly around and connect with each other when we smile, causing us to feel better. Then they write long and complicated "dissertations" and "thesis" (words themselves tire me just looking at them) that would bore most of us to death, causing someone like me to try to summarize their many years of work, in a few short sentences... Author David Brooks helps me further summarize by saying, "Over the past few years, geneticists, neuroscientists, psychologists, sociologists, economists, anthropologists, and others have made great strides in understanding the building blocks of human flourishing." (Brooks, 2012, p. VIII)

I believe the current scientific findings about human nature are *revolutionary*[14]. They hold the key to unlocking the door to become your best self, and also to helping fix America's problems. I will explain how.

A. The incredibly strong and mysterious powers of the human brain: The power of our brains is almost *incomprehensible*[15]. In The Secret Power of Babies, Dr. Danihane Stanihouse writes that at the time of our birth we "already possess considerable knowledge inherited from its long evolutionary history... the scope of babies' prior knowledge is extensive." We are born with a vast repertoire of abilities... Objects, numbers, probabilities, faces, language... Even just a few hours after birth a baby can recognize and react to a smiling face... From birth on, our brain is already endowed with intuitive logic." and a "... stunningly sophisticated knack for applying observed knowledge". Experiments show that we "possess a remarkable capacity to acquire grammar in a remarkable time. What is hardwired in them (babies) is not so much language itself but the ability to acquire it". The article goes on to say how babies immediately know the difference between if an animal moves because it's alive versus a non-living object. We do things with blocks and balloons that you wouldn't believe! In his article, "All we do is Learn," Richard Jerome says,

> "...by subconscious imitation, human beings are multifaceted learning machines from our first days to our last. [We have] complex

---

14. revolutionary: involving or causing a complete or dramatic change.
15. incomprehensible: not able to be understood; not intelligible

neurological supercomputers housed in our skulls…" We hoover up data, ideas, behaviors, and all manner of stimuli from day one, and we learn when we are not even aware we are learning… All of this learning… involves an elaborate biochemical choreography performed by neurons, synapses, and neurotransmitters- a process that remains largely mysterious'… How else, for example, does one account for someone such as Leslie Lemke, The blind Wisconsin pianist, who has performed all over the world? He has low verbal IQ of 58 and suffers from cerebral palsy. Yet Lemke can listen to a piece of music once through, and no matter how intricate the work, play it back with unerring precision… Lemke has never taken a music lesson in his life! Another unschooled sculptor, Alonzo Clemens, 63, can glance at an animal for a few seconds and mold a clay replica that is essentially exact in every detail, down to the last muscle and tendon… Psychiatrists say that these extraordinary people 'possess a genetic memory,' a kind of chip in their brains that gives them not only natural skills but innate access to the rules of art, math, music, and even language in the absence of any formal training… this chip of sophisticated knowledge comes factory installed." (Jerome, 2021)

Take Benjamin Franklin, one of my idols as another example. He's the guy who invented electricity with no formal education. "Mr. Franklin's education had not opened up for him a career in the sciences, but nature had given him a genius for them. His first attempts regarding electricity reveal that he knew very little even on that part of physics… he had only imperfect experimental tools. However, he soon surmised the immediate cause of electrical phenomena." (Ansart, 2015) He would later go on to rally the hopes and dreams of hundreds of thousands of people, many of lesser natural-born intelligence, by writing in ways that they respected. These writings helped form America. All skills that he was born with. Of course, all brains are not created equal, they develop at different speeds, and some naturally have more tolerances and capacities than others.

Doctors agree that *genetics*[16] and some luck play a role.

While it may be true that we are not all born with the intellectual capacity of BenFranklin -I'm hopeful that you can pick up what I am laying down- **we are born with mad skills!** The fact is that we are surrounded by countless more brilliant people than we are not.

B. We are all born with a seed of natural goodness planted in our hearts and souls.

I don't know about you, but I can't look at a bunch of newborn babies in the hospital, sucking on their binkies, holding onto their blankies, and thinking, "Woe is me, look at all those future troublemakers." I mean what type of society would we have if we thought that people are, by nature, flawed? Wouldn't we put up our guard and be fearful? This would be a horrible way to live. I've always believed in the natural goodness of people and that we come into this world with traits, such as optimism, kindness, and tolerance as standard equipment. But there is SO much more to this. Luckily for all of us, there is more to this than just my opinion. The idea that all human beings are born with good intentions and that our good traits far outweigh our bad ones, at least at the time of our birth, is well supported by modern science.

In a recent study, in the 2019 book, *Compassionomics*, Doctors Trzeciak and Mazzarelli have proven in their research that "toddlers are naturally inclined to altruistically help others" (Mazzarelli, and Trzeciak). (*Altruistic[17]*) *and that* "Compassion is intrinsic to the human condition." We are born with it. They define compassion as *"the emotional response to another's pain or suffering, involving an authentic desire to help."* Compassion is one of the most important words in our language. It's different from *empathy*[18] (another important word) which is, they say "the feeling and understanding component. Compassion involves

---

16. genetics: the study of heredity and the variation of inherited characteristics
17. altruistic: showing a disinterested and selfless concern for the well-being of others; unselfish
18. empathy: the ability to understand and share the feelings of another

taking action...think of it like this; empathy hurts, but compassion heals. Some people's fire for compassion, love, and kindness is raging when they are born and this fire never goes out. Others are born with less, but each of us has at least a spark. Please hold onto this fact as you grow up, because people will start to disappoint you. You need to understand that they weren't born to be bad. Seeing the world through this fundamental prism of truth will help your generation take our country to a better place. If nothing else, remember that all human beings are born with goodness in our souls. That is the best thing about being human, and it's another fact about us, that is undeniable. More on this later.

C. **We are more capable of overcoming adversity, coping, and adapting than we think:**

"The wiring in our brains is not fixed- it's adaptable," says Dr. Richard Davidson. It can adapt and change with a "remarkably short amount of practice." (Davidson, 2012) This may sound like a weak attempt to be positive just for positivity's sake- but it's far from that! Dr. Daniel Amen, an MD and the founder of Amen Clinics has spent his life studying the human brain, particularly how it responds to different types of events and circumstances. At the time of this writing, he and his team have looked at over 83,000 brain scans- detailed pictures of our brains. Each one the subject of a certain condition such as trauma. Among his conclusions are that "we are not stuck with the brain that we have" (Amen, 2008). After a setback, or after feeling sad or being rejected we can renew and regain our powers.

Of the various types of doctors who study how the brain works, there are those who focus on how we best learn (or not). Dr. Eva Kyndt has spent years researching how we best learn. She says, "The question, 'How does our brain work?', is very similar to How does our brain learn? Motivation or a willingness to learn is one of the most essential ingredients to learning. The brain doesn't hold onto information arbitrarily, it keeps what it believes it can use."

I interpret what she is saying here as being related to the concept or idea of willpower. Others call it being mentally tough. Say you are at Dunkin Donuts staring down your fourth donut, you can either say to yourself, 'I don't have the skills right now to decline that donut.' Or you can decide to obtain the skills in that moment to NOT take the donut! If you value the decision you are making deeply enough, you can distance yourself from your first impulse, to form the intention to not have the donut. But if you don't think that decision is important enough if you fail to focus hard enough, your brain is going to blow you off... and you will be chowing down in the next second. Donuts, Butternut, Coffee rolls... Chocolate Frosted Glazed... are SO good. I go through this process on most days.

Ms. Carol Dweck, Ph.D., teaches at Stanford University. Her research concludes that the brain does its best learning in the process of failing and trying again. She writes, "Stretching yourself and sticking to it, even (or especially) when it's not going well, is the hallmark of a growth mindset. This is the mindset that allows people to thrive during some of the most challenging times in their lives." (Dweck). She says that the process of learning is far more important than the result. Therefore, if you get a bad grade on an exam, the worst thing you can do for your future is to shut down, think that you are stupid, and run away from it. The more we challenge our brains to work through difficult choices and problems in our lives, the stronger our brains become. If you stop believing you will not accomplish your goals. The decisions you make after having failed will be the most important ones you make in your life.

I remember my daughter Katelin, who is now 26 years old, going through some very hard times, from about 7th to 9th grade. There were a lot of tears shed during that time of her life, as she transitioned from middle school to high school. She seemed to be competing for relationships, status, coaches' attention, etc. Questioning things and doubting yourself is totally normal and it's very hard for you to know that the tears you shed now, once dried, are helping you grow into finding yourself. Similar to horses at the start of the Kentucky Derby, all fighting to find their positions, dirt is kicked up and thrown in their faces, but they eventually settle in and find their "stride." You too will find yours. Remember- You are more "resilient" than you think. The more dirt we have kicked in our faces, that we wipe off the stronger we become. It's how we handle our feelings, after our letdowns, that will ultimately change the course of our lives. Katelin today says that she "can't believe" the things that she used to let bother her, and I know that she would report to you a similar message that Robert Frost, a great American poet once said, "In three words I can sum up everything I've learned about life- It goes on."

Quick story, and example of a changed mindset. I coached both my boys in little league, and when Johnny was in the major league I remember I had a kid named Billy Welton, whose father was always barking at him, giving him instructions as he stepped into the batters' box. I could tell it was freaking Billy out. He was also striking out a lot. I could almost feel his father's disappointment, so I could only imagine how Billy felt. I decided to try something, first I made sure to keep his dad behind the fence. Then I approached Billy with a smile on my face, grabbing him on the shoulders, and looking into his big blue eyes. I said to Billy ``Do me a favor... just smile." He had a great smile. "Now Billy when the ball is coming in at you, keep smiling," I said. Well, he did, and wouldn't you know Billy hit a homerun. I do not make that up. As Oprah Winfrey wisely said, "The greatest discovery of all time is that a person can change his future by merely changing his attitude." (Winfrey) So remember, science proves that the more we overcome, the better we get at it. In the face of a difficult problem, a test at school, a relationship problem, don't give up, no matter what. You will thrive if you hang in there, and make it through the low moments that we all have.

You may be wondering why I'm giving you these facts in a book about politics. I'm hopeful that the reason will become clear to you very soon. Please get a snack or something if you need to because this next Chapter needs to be fully digested, but before turning the page, do me a favor- smile.

Thank you.

Chapter 2: Human Nature- The Not So Good News

There is an "Elephant in the Room" we need to talk about... Envision a 4000-pound elephant sitting in a room with a bunch of people discussing a problem, and everyone pretends not to notice the elephant! Sorta funny, right? The Elephant in the room is an old expression that you may have heard. It's the thing everyone avoids talking about when, in fact, it is **the** most important thing **to** talk about. When it comes to our brains, the expression has never been more fitting.

About our brains, as incredibly strong as they are, they are equally as complicated, and that's putting it nicely. It's actually worse than that. Weirdly enough, scientists say that we have a negativity bias. We are prone to think more negatively than positively, and our brains are also naturally wired to constantly feed us unwanted negative thoughts, which lead to self-doubt. When we get into a negative train of thought which we often do, our brains tend to reinforce that pattern unless we know how to break the cycle. Our brains have a tendency to send us information that we didn't ask for, and if we aren't cognizant, and don't remain *vigilant*[19], the misinformation it sends us causes us to think in distorted ways. In fact, Doctors call the tricks our brains play on us cognitive distortions, and there are some real *doozies*[20]. It's different for every person, of course, but let me borrow from the experts because my intent is not to scare you. Rather, it is to provide you with information that I believe can help save us.

Dr. Jonathan Haidt, one of America's leading psychologists (and one of the smartest people I've ever come across, at least as evidenced by his writings), studies the inner workings of our brains and explains our condition in ways which help us prepare and overcome. Doctor Haidt earned his Ph.D. in psychology in 1992. At the time of this writing, he is a Professor of Ethical Leadership at New York University (NYU). Prior to that, he taught Introduction to Psychology at the University of Virginia.

---

19. vigilant: keeping careful watch for possible danger or difficulties
20. doozy: something outstanding or unique of its kind

He is a leading expert in the growing field of positive psychology, a field that is committed to teaching all of us how we can stay mentally fit and emotionally well.

He writes, "One of the greatest truths in psychology is that the mind is divided into parts that sometimes conflict. To be human is to feel pulled in different directions, and to marvel -sometimes in horror- at your inability to control your own actions." In writing about what he calls our divided mind, Dr. Haidt describes roadblocks to our well-being that our minds place in front of us, and which are hard to navigate unless we become more aware. To explain how and why this happens he provides a powerful *metaphor*[21]- "The image that I came up with for myself, as I marveled at my weakness, was that I was a rider on the back of an elephant. I'm holding the reins in my handles and by pulling one way or the other I can tell the elephant to turn, to stop or go. I can direct things, but only when the elephant doesn't have desires of his own. When the elephant really wants to do something, I'm no match for him." (Haidt, 2013)

The elephant, he says, represents our emotional and automatic systems, and he is the big guy on the block. The rider, on the other hand, represents our rational and analytical systems, and he is much smaller. Apparently, the elephant part of our brain is much older and far more developed than the little rider, who from an evolutionary standpoint, is a relative newbie still learning how to do his job. The elephant side of our brain runs on immediate impulses. The rider tries to apply logic or rational cause-and-effect thinking, often without success. The rider obeys the speed limit while the elephant stomps on the gas. The elephant loves to party and will rage all night, while the rider wants to leave early and take an Uber. (the smart decision!).

The elephant's behaviors are so deeply embedded into us when an impulse or temptation feels good, it feels REAL good. The Elephant enjoys challenging rules and causing trouble, and even raising a bit of hell. Our first thoughts and immediate impulses ALWAYS come from the elephant. The big guy speaks first for us. You may have heard the comment, "think before you speak", that is the rider trying to pull in on our reins, so we don't say

---

21. metaphor: a figure of speech in which a word or phrase is applied to an object or action to which it is not literally applicable

anything stupid. The elephant represents our hot systems, and wants to run hot- wild and free. The rider represents our cooling systems. For example, the rider would be the one who gets us to the gym to exercise, whereas the elephant never wants to go, but if we do get there what is the first thing we do? We blast music into our ears. We do this to distract the rider and to fire up that powerful elephant inside of us. Give it a try- push yourself, engage the fiery passion of your elephant side of you. Just be careful to engage enough of your little rider so you don't fall off the treadmill, or drop a weight on your foot.

There is a deep and *profound*[22] dueling element which is playing out constantly between our emotions (the elephant) and our reasoning (the rider). Between this duel, Dr. Haidt says that "the elephant is vastly stronger, and tends to win any conflict that arises between the two… the rider generally functions more like the elephant's servant than its master." He says "We often use reasoning <u>not to find the truth but to invent arguments to support our deep intuitive beliefs residing in the elephant</u>" (Haidt, 2006). "the rider is extremely skilled at producing *post-hoc*[23] justifications for whatever he does or believes." He writes, "The rider interprets what is happening in ways that are consistent with the elephant's emotional state, <u>without investigating what is true</u>. The rider acts like a lawyer or press secretary whose job it is to rationalize and justify the elephant's "pre-ordained" conclusions, rather than to inquire into- or even be curious about- what is really true." (Lukianoff; Haidt, 2019). My interpretation of what he is saying is that we are basically prone to toss logic out the window, so long as our emotions are satisfied.

These are the facts of the human brain; divided by sides which are constantly fighting: Slow/Fast- Start/Stop- Left/Right- pulling, twisting, questioning each other, and on and on. Welcome to being human.

I have been amazed, and scared at times, at how I've seen this play out in my own mind. In fact, my own experiences with unwanted negative thoughts and self-doubt are reasons why I am writing this book. I will explain this in more detail in Chapter

---

22. profound: of a state, quality, or emotion) very great or intense
23. posthoc: after the fact and made up

Ten. I seem to have survived it- so far- as most of us do, but it hasn't been easy for me. I consider myself lucky to have learned how to cope and deal with my divided mind but I put in the required work pretty much every day. Many adults are not so lucky- This is what explains most of what is happening in America today.

Don't believe me? Consider just one other thing that science says about us. The researchers say that we are naturally prone to form groups and will fight till the end to protect our traditions, similar to how bees fight to their death to protect their queen, the elephant inside of us loves to rally around a cause or a person. That is, Dr. Haidt says that people are born with natural instincts to take sides and become *hyperpartisan*. Sounds a little like clubs, gangs, and our political parties, doesn't it?

Now imagine 32 million Wild Elephants running loose in our society... with riders who have lost control. Sounds about right, huh?*

So what are we to make of all of this? Can we solve societal problems by knowing more about how we are all hardwired and the vulnerabilities we all share as humans? Yes, we can!

The challenge we face in organizing a society of millions of humans is the most complicated problem ever created by mankind. The work of *citizenship*[24] is not easy, in fact, that is the largest understatement in this book. Deciding who is in need and dividing stuff up among fellow citizens is extremely complicated. We are constantly being asked to make compromises that we don't want to make and give up things we desire for people we don't even know. The limitations imposed by the government on individual *freedoms*[25]- and *regulations*[26] would annoy the heck out of any elephant! Given all of this, it should come as no surprise that we are fighting like common animals over rules-related stuff.

---

24. citizenship: the position or status of being a citizen of a particular country
25. freedoms: the power or right to act, speak, or think as one wants without hindrance or restraint
26. regulation: a rule or directive made and maintained by an authority

I want this information to linger, like a bad fart... My editor asked me to remove the part about this smelling like a fart... two times. But I couldn't take it out. The truth about how humans are naturally prone to think is too important. With that in mind, please take a deep breath in... smell our reality. These facts about our human nature ARE the key to improving our society, but, for reasons we are about to explore, we have heretofore failed to approach the challenges of living together in a shared society with people who are different from us with the right foundation of knowledge.

Please bookmark the two photos on the next page.

---

*32 Million is 10% of 320 Million which is the rough population of the USA.- Referencing my 10% theory, that only about 10% lose their battle with their divided mind.

In this first image, the two divided parts of the brain are working together. The rider is squarely balanced on top of his elephant, steering the large animal into a wedding ceremony. Each is drawing on the other's strengths. These are our 90%er's, capable of dealing with the complex problems that society throws at us. We might call these people-centered or balanced.

The other picture (the bucking bronco) represents a person who has *succumbed*[27] to his divided mind. As you see in the picture,

---

27. succumb: fail to resist pressure or temptation

he is being tossed and thrown by the larger and more mature part of his nature. Please just replace the bronco with an elephant in your mind. The elephant part of his brain is getting the best of the rider. These are our 10%ers.

We might call our 10%ers, a little off-kilter, askew, off-center, out of line, outlandish, erratic, far-out, spaced out, kooky, or bizarro... but we don't call them names to put them down, that is the worst thing we can do. We need to love these individuals, but we need to spot them to be able to see how they impact us, particularly in what they are doing to our politics. These people are definitely fun to party with. I keep them in my contact book for parties, but when it comes to helping us solve the most complex challenges of our society their abilities are *suboptimal*[28]. Without retraining, they lack the abilities needed of a citizen, such as evenness of temper, but they lack a lot more than that. If being reasonable, and staying calm in the face of adversity was a business they would be closed. We have to figure out if they are too far gone or if we can somehow get them to change their ways and fix our political problems... From here on out, I will refer to them affectionately as our "Bucking Broncos".

In case you are wondering, if you are under the age of 25, you likely remain in the 90% group. Congratulations! See, like most forms of decay such as mold and rot, they do not form immediately. It only happens given time and exposure to certain conditions. Like a flower that doesn't get what it needs, it wilts. Think for a moment, about what I will refer to as the "potted plant comparison". Imagine the "soil" the plant is sitting in as "parenting." The "water" it needs is formal "schooling," and the "sunshine"- is everything else including positive social experiences, and making and sustaining human connections. At a basic level, every person needs decent soil to grow proper roots, followed by water and sunshine. We can begin to understand how people lose the battle, by not getting enough of these things. Sadly, failure to receive ample amounts of these ingredients can cause us to *degenerate*[29] and become *ignorant*[30].

---

28. suboptimal: of less than the highest standard or quality
29. degenerate: having lost the physical, mental, or moral qualities considered normal and desirable; showing evidence of decline.
30. ignorant: lacking knowledge or awareness in general; uneducated

At this point, all I ask of you is to remember two very important things:

> 1. Ignorance alone is what is causing all the undesired outcomes in our society.
> 2. The people who are behaving this way- it is not their fault. The fact is- "Everyone you meet is fighting a battle you know nothing about" Ian Maclaren.

This concludes the not so good news.

Chapter 3: The Many Paths to Greatness

In the first two chapters, we learned that science has a lot to say about us. However, as important as science is, it doesn't explain everything. In fact, science doesn't come close to explaining how incredible we are. I've traveled widely across our country, built schools in the poorest of neighborhoods, the urban and the suburban, and have met people from all walks of life. It is clear to me that aside from a few hard political issues that can be unwrapped, (soon) the great majority of us are not behaving like stupid animals… This is despite what Dr. Haidt and his friends say about us. (Sorry, Dr. Haidt, I still love you. Please keep the science coming!). I think I've figured out how this is happening. The fact is that while we may be animals, we are beautiful animals. We draw upon things such as hope, optimism, and spirituality like no other species, to lift us from our lowest lows and propel us to our highest highs.

There is no substitute for hope and optimism. Of all the mysterious things in life, they are the most powerful tools we have to get what we want out of our lives. When applied often, hope and optimism tame our proneness for negativity and self-doubt. Even that darn elephant listens to hope and optimism. And for many of us, there is a fine line between hope and optimism and something even more powerful – a higher level. I call it the spiritual realm. There are times in my life when I feel blessed with superb skills, untouchable, confident, and courageous, but not in a selfish way, in a giving way. It is in these moments when I feel incredibly healthy, in mind and *spirit*[31]. I feel a force, greater than myself, inside me, helping me to achieve such a positive outlook. This is why I choose to believe that there is something out there, a higher power of some kind that is driving things, and on which I can rely.

But before I start talking about what you think I may be talking about -and you are correct, it's "God", I want to keep your eye on the prize and make this chapter about only one thing I've figured out how and why my 90% rule is accurate. It is because there are many different paths people take to develop the virtues

---

31. spirit: the nonphysical part of a person which is the seat of emotions and character; the soul

to be a good person as well as the qualities to be good citizens!

There are traditional paths that involve having the right mix of parenting, schooling, and social experiences. This is the "potted plant" comparison which I talked about in Chapter One. This might also be called the prescriptive path because it's like a doctor simply writes a prescription, and you follow the instructions. For example, "Squeeze the tube and rub the lotion on your bum- bum, three times daily." And it works! Today if you Google "what makes a person happy" there will be pages of prescriptive-type articles full of these *antidotes*[32]. They may sound *cliche*[33] or overused to you, but for the most part, it's all good guidance- if you can follow it.

Then there is the spiritual path, which nobody can explain to us, but we feel it in our soul; a connection to something larger that is just out there waiting for us to discover- maybe after this life, and these beliefs give us strength to power through. This element has played a huge role in my life, and I believe it plays a big role for many of us.

Then there is another category of people altogether, which in my mind, reveals the most about human nature. I'm speaking of people who grow up with little of the traditional nourishments, nor do they rely on faith, yet somehow they manage to develop a strong faith in themselves. The road they follow may be best defined as one of "struggle, endurance, and redemption."

In many cases, these folks start out with almost nothing to be hopeful or optimistic about. If this is you right now, please keep reading because people who are living this path very often don't realize what is coming of them, but something incredible is happening. By being forced to overcome obstacles and size up their fears, they leave them in the dust. These people are the ones that, in my mind, demonstrate best how special and amazing human beings are. I was very lucky to have someone in my life who traveled this road. He was my father, and a bit of his story is worth telling.

---

32. antidote: a medicine taken or given to counteract a particular poison
33. cliche: a phrase or opinion that is overused and betrays a lack of original thought

Arthur H. Cort was born in Boston in 1919 into a very poor single-parent home. His mother, Lillian, would leave the family for long stretches at a time, basically abandoning him. So my dad and his older sister Selma had to live in temporary state-run foster care. His father, Jack, was a warm, *jovial*[34] and loving man who did his best to keep the kids under his roof but sadly was unable to because he worked full-time as a plumber.

My dad didn't tell us too much about his childhood, but there is one story that I recall about the man who took them in for a short period of time when he was a teenager. "His name was Beeeeersohn..." my dad would say, always in an animated sort of way and stretching out the vowels. "He had a hunch in his back, used a cane or a stick, and walked with a limp. I was dreadfully fearful of this man", he reported. Whatever difficulty my father had growing up, he shielded most of it from his kids. I guess he didn't want to burden us with his grief. Rather he wanted to give us a childhood unlike his. In fact, he would always make light of the challenges of his youth. When he told the "Bearson" story later in his life, he would add softening elements to the story, such as, "the old man may have been a wonderfully kind person, just doing the best he could," even though it was clearly a terrible experience for him. He must have been a very scared little boy. Yet all we could get out of him about his adolescent years was, "I went to the school of hard knocks."

I never heard my dad utter a bad word about his mother. In fact, later in life, I remember his efforts to take his mother in and support her when no one else would. "Nana" died in the room across the hall from me when I was eight or nine years old, as my father sought to mend relations. She seemed nice enough. Although my parents made me give her a kiss every night before bedtime, and these were not the best of times for me. Her chin felt a bit hairy, to be honest... which may explain what is wrong with me, but that's another story altogether...

It is unclear if my father graduated high school, but we do know that he read the dictionary as a teenager. He kept it next to his

---

34. jovial: cheerful and friendly

bed for years, as well as a *thesaurus*.[35] My father taught himself the English language. He tried pharmacy school as a young man but couldn't afford it, so in 1942, at the age of 19, he enlisted in the Army.

He didn't tell us too much about his military experience, but it became obvious that it was important to shaping the man that he would become. His group was the first to arrive when the prisoners were *liberated*[36] from the Nazi *concentration camps*[37] in Dachau, Germany. The prisoners had to be *de-loused*[38] by a process of throwing powdered antibiotics onto them to remove the lice. My Dad sent pictures of the process along with piles of dead bodies to his brother, my Uncle Billy, back home, who shared the pictures of us when we were old enough to look at

them. My dad had to also remove the dead bodies and load them onto trucks, all before the age of 25. Pictured here is my dad when he enlisted.

In 1945, when the war ended, returning soldiers were allowed a certain amount of surplus goods, which they obtained by lottery at the Army Office of War Assets in Boston at 10 Kneeland Street (today's

35. thesaurus: a resource that lists words in groups of <u>synonyms</u> and related concepts
36. liberated: (of a place or people) freed from imprisonment, slavery, or enemy occupation
37. concentration camp: a place where large numbers of people, especially political prisoners or members of persecuted minorities, are deliberately imprisoned in a relatively small area with inadequate facilities, sometimes to provide forced labor or to await mass execution. The term is most strongly associated with the several hundred camps established by the Nazis in Germany and occupied Europe in 1933–45, among the most infamous being Dachau, Belsen, and Auschwitz
38. de-loused: to remove lice from

Chinatown). My father focused on tires and other auto parts but soon had another focus, who sat at a certain desk working as a government administrator on the second floor. After making small talk with a young lady named Marie Chappelle for a while, he would eventually drop her a note that read, "What does a guy like me have to do to go out with a gal like you?" My dad had a good rap! From that moment, it was game on and game over. My Mom and Dad fell in love and would eventually get married.

The images of his early years before settling down are right out of a movie set from that era. He lived quite literally on the streets of the inner city, "bouncing around," as he would say, selling his army surplus door to door to small trucking companies and doing other odd jobs to "make ends meet." They played stickball well into the night, white tee shirts, black pants, leather shoes, and all!

He also hung around the billiards halls, "pool sharking," said my Uncle Bill. Your dad "shot one-handed and learned how to place 'English' on the ball !" (which I have learned is spin). "He was a hustler and won more often than he lost." When I was older, hanging out at the horse track (Suffolk Downs in East Boston), his best friend Skippy, who looked like a gangster, by the way… haha, would remind me, "Your dad was a tough guy- nobody messed around with your father." I suppose that felt good to hear, but my father never came across to me as hard-nosed or tough in that way. In fact, from what I could tell, he never used his masculinity as a weapon. Rather, my dad was the *epitome*[39] of a real gentleman.

Quick ending story about my dad: When he retired to Florida, he owned a boat. During one of my visits, I recall a boat mechanic named Joe spent what seemed like every day of the whole week at the house. As it turned out, Joe wasn't a very good mechanic. I recall witnessing a conversation between my dad and Joe. While being presented with an invoice and with a boat still unable to leave the dock, I could see my Dad struggling with the situation. Joe had failed my father in every way, not only in that he couldn't explain the problem with the boat, but he was stumbling to explain his invoice too. My father said to him, "Joe, don't worry about it. You tried your best, and some problems are very

39. epitome: a person or thing that is a perfect example of a particular quality or type

complex. We will live to fight another day." It was important for my father to allow Joe to save his honor or not be embarrassed by the circumstances. He also probably knew that Joe would get into trouble if he failed to collect the money. I witnessed this type of thing all the time. My dad placed the courteous treatment of other people at the center of his life.

No one ever said a negative word about my dad, except maybe my mom, of course …but that is to be expected in a marriage of 54 years… Haha. This photo is of my mom and dad on their wedding day.

Many people have gone to great lengths to study and write about this road of struggle and endurance. In his book, *The Road to Character*, author David Brooks writes, "We are all stumblers… The stumbler scuffs through life, a little off balance here and there, sometimes lurching, sometimes falling to her knees. But the stumbler faces her imperfect nature, her mistakes and weaknesses, with unvarnished honesty... But humility offers self-understanding... The stumbler is made whole by this struggle. Each weakness becomes a chance to wage a campaign that is organized and gives meaning to life and makes you a better person...through internal struggle and a sense of their own limitations, they have built a strong inner character...each struggle leaves a residue...A person who has gone through these struggles seems more substantial and deep. By magic *alchemy[40]*, these victories turn weakness into joy... Joy is a byproduct experienced by people who are aiming for something else. But it comes."(Brooks, 2015, p. 268). This was my father- a *by-product[41]* of a process.

I remember he said to me one time, "Son, life begins at 40." (my dad was 49 years old when I was born) I will never forget that. By the time I knew my father, he had come out on the other side of this process. I saw plenty of joy in his eyes, but I can't speak to his internal joy as much as I can to his greatness as a patriarch, a leader, and now as I reflect upon our failing society, as a tax-paying citizen. He was the perfect blend of confidence and *humility.[42]* He never exaggerated his own abilities or caused anyone to think that he was better than them. He was fiercely *resolute[43]* in his business and had success, employing hundreds of people. Back then, you might call him a politician when it still had a positive meaning attached to it. He wasn't flashy, but he was far from boring. He didn't finish high school, and he didn't go to college. But as I said, he read the dictionary and developed an incredible way with words. It was the way that he worked on communicating effectively and with other people that I remember most about him. Through effective communication, he bridged differences between people. This, I believe, is his most lasting legacy to me, and I hope mine to you.

---

40. alchemy: a seemingly magical process of transformation, creation or combination
41. by-product: an incidental or secondary product made in the manufacture or synthesis of something else
42. humility: a modest or low view of one's own importance; humbleness
43. resolute: admirably purposeful, determined, and unwavering

Have you ever heard the expression, "Be the bigger person"? If you haven't, that is ok. What is more important is that we learn how to become one. The "bigger person" places the burden on themselves to communicate in a way to cause a fair outcome for all involved. In the face of disagreement, the bigger person responds with manners, *grace*[44], *and politeness*[45]." They work hard to consider perspectives other than their own. They give others the benefit of the doubt and allow adversaries *to* "save face." Importantly, this doesn't make them a pushover, as some would have you believe. It's actually the opposite. The bigger person is always the most persuasive in the room, and you will never hear a bigger person raise their voice- they don't have to in order to be heard. The bigger person can stay calm when needed most.

I have recently come to realize that maintaining peace in our country requires a great effort by each of us to develop these skills, to learn how to maintain a certain *disposition*[46]. To have patience for people with whom we disagree and to become "gentlemanly" in our manner. It seems more important than ever that we help your generation figure out how to gain these skills and maintain them when faced with someone you disagree with and even with whom you dislike. If everyone we ever interacted with could do these things- we could accomplish our goals. But how do we get there?

The good news is, as I said, there are many paths. Dr. Walter Mischel wrote a now famous book called The Marshmallow Test that placed marshmallows (and cookies) in front of young kids and clocked how long each kid could delay their gratification (as the Dr. says) and not eat the marshmallow. Wouldn't you know, the kids who could delay the longest, either by distraction or mind control, turned out to achieve more in their life? "At age 27-32, those who had waited longer during the Marshmallow Test in preschool had... a better sense of self-worth, pursued their goals more effectively, and coped more adaptively with frustration and stress. At midlife, those who could consistently wait, versus those who couldn't, were characterized by

---

44. grace: simple elegance or refinement of movement
45. politeness: behavior that is respectful and considerate of other people
46. disposition: a person's inherent qualities of mind and character

distinctively different brain scans in areas linked to addictions and obesity." (Mischel, 2014, p. 5)

To not seek glory, to defer credit, to be more patient, to open the door for people, and let others go first rather than rush in. To voluntarily eat last at the buffet, and to take less -even though you want more. To consider our own faults daily, to wonder how we can be better. I know that none of this sounds like fun, but it has been proven to create bigger people rather than smaller ones.

You must be wondering, as I have, must I suffer to become a happy, fulfilled person and a good citizen? Well, the short answer is, in part– sorta. Let me explain. Basically, we all experience bad and unpleasant things in our lives. The universe simply throws a lot at us. If you are sitting at home right now and your parents are fighting, you know what I mean. If you've been bullied on social media, have been called a loser, or you've gone through a breakup you know what I mean. If you didn't make the team, or recently failed a test and didn't think you had the smarts to cut it, you know what I mean. We all experience a certain amount of sadness and frustration in our lives, and sometimes it takes us to a very low place. And as we learned in Chapter One, our brains tend to cause us to think the worst unless we decide to break the cycle. Science, such as the marshmallow test and others, are the tools that teach us how to stay on the path to greatness.

Luckily, suffering through childhood is **not** a prerequisite to having a great life. Life isn't that cruel. I had a much different upbringing than my father did. I grew up with nutrient-rich "soil" (supportive and loving parents) with steady "watering" (formal schooling), and I was extremely lucky to have a lot of sunshine in my life in the form of friends. My father grew up with sub-par "soil" and almost no "water"... Looking back on things, I realize now that my father and I only had one thing in common, the "Sunshine" piece. Our childhoods were defined by thousands of hand-to-hand, and eye-to-eye interactions that were dynamic, warm, challenging, hard, and fun. We both grew up outside.

My mom wouldn't let us ever sit around the house and watch TV. We had a huge bus stop for years, and we would always show up an hour early to play hide-n-seek. We made "slingshots" out of rubber bands, rode dirt bikes, made fires in the woods, and pegged houses with rotten apples (only once?). All of the houses in the neighborhood had large outdoor bells which parents would ring (by pulling a long string which

activated the steel mechanism inside the chamber) to get us home for dinner. I lived more than a mile from the high school, and you could hear the bell from the upper fields. Someone was always being scolded for being late.

My brother Jack was very popular when we were growing up. He was two years older than me. He was very well-liked and had a lot of friends. My mom would say that he had movie star looks. He looked like a young George Clooney (I'm not sure if you are old enough to know who that is) As Jack's little brother, I received a lot of attention from upperclassmen in High school. Jack's friends used to pick on me, but not in a mean way, more in a way that just tested my mettle. They threw me into the scum-filled pond behind the school. They shoved straw down my underwear and hung me on a hook on the back of the town Fire Station. (of all places, right?) Back then, they called this giving someone a Wedgie.

I'm surprised that Siri actually knows what a Wedgie is, given I'm not sure kids give them any more? But Siri actually had a definition for it when I asked her- *"the act of forcibly pulling a person's underpants upwards from the back."*

and even provided a picture of one on Wikipedia. (shown here). I guess Siri thinks wedgies are still a thing.

At the time, it didn't seem like these experiences were helping me in any way. In fact, the wedgie still hurts today! Looking back on my life, I have come to realize we learn more from hard times than we are able to realize in the moment. I'm convinced making and keeping so many friends has saved me.

The guys who hung me on the hook behind the fire station became some of my best friends. I was my brother Jack's "Best Man" for his wedding and arranged the bachelor party. We had nearly SIXTY friends fly from all over the country to Las Vegas for the event! I ran it like a large wedding. We piled into two suites, and I rented a donkey and snuck it into the hotel. The event was over twenty years ago, but I still run into people in Boston who remind me, in their Boston accent, of "the best party EVAH!," and they beg me to have a reunion -I hope I can make that happen someday. But seriously, I want to thank my brother for helping me form so many great friendships. It doesn't always come easy, and I have been lucky to make and keep many close friendships. It has proven to have a direct bearing on my happiness. There may be a few more Vegas stories later in the book, but for this, I may need a separate chapter on Political Correctness!

So the question is, do you need to have sixty people at your bachelor or bachelorette party to be a happy and fulfilled person? Yes, you do... but you don't have to rent the Donkey like I did. I'm kidding, of course, but let's balance the kidding with our being laser-focused on the point being made here- The quality of our connections in life equals the quality of our outlook.

The great Aristotle said, "Men are not isolated individuals... human excellences cannot be practiced by hermits." Nat Rutherford, Professor of political theory at the University of London, who writes, "For Aristotle, we flourish by exercising our uniquely human capabilities to think and reason. But thinking and reasoning are as much social activities as they are individual... Our flourishing originates from and arises from our relationships with others. Happiness is not an emotional state so much as it is the excellence of the relations we cultivate with other people.' (Rutherford, 2022) In their book *Compassionomics*, Dr. Trzexiak writes, "Human connection is strongly associated with human health" (Mazzarelli & Trzeciak, 2019). The XYZ study tracked over 20,000 teens into young adulthood and looked at "four measures of physical health: body mass index, inflammation, abdominal weight, and blood pressure." The study concluded, "With each additional social connection that you have, you get an added beneficial effect for your health... the more, the better... The fewer social connections the person had, the poorer their health, and vice versa."

These connections greatly impact our ability to regulate our emotions and deal with the many pressures of life- AND this, as I will show you later in the book, directly correlates to our being able to get along in our politics. Maybe that's it- we should start giving wedgies to all of our congressmen. Don't I wish it was that simple?

I just got off the phone with an old high school friend we called "Baloose." Baloose lived dangerously, and I don't want to encourage you to do things that will cause you danger, but I'm having trouble thinking back on the things that Baloose and I did together that weren't a bit dangerous. He climbed trees so high you couldn't see him. He jumped in ponds while golfers were teeing off and yelling at him. He lived like part monkey and part superhero. He was locked up a few times but for nothing serious. (Sorry Baloose) Today, he is a very successful businessman now living in Japan with a loving wife and two great kids, with vacation homes in Thailand and Hawaii.

The scientific research is also telling us that when we are young, we need to "engage in thousands of hours of play, including thousands of falls, scrapes, conflicts, insults, alliances, betrayals, status competitions, and acts of exclusion... (Haidt & Lukianoff, 2018, p. 183) These interactions, even the ones that might make you sad, or cry, help you practice dealing with things like frustration, boredom, and conflict. This is the key to your development. "If we protect children (you) from various classes of potentially upsetting experiences we make it far more likely that those children will be unable to cope with such events when they leave our protective umbrella. The modern obsession with protecting young people from feeling unsafe is we believe one of the (several) causes of the rapid rise in rates of adolescent depression, anxiety, and suicide."(Haidt & Lukianoff, 2018, p. 24) So this is serious stuff, but I promised I wouldn't lecture you in this book. Like to get off the couch, put the gaming controller down, and remove your face from your phone! If you are reading this book, you are way ahead of the game, so I won't do that… But seriously, do me a favor: Get off the couch, put the gaming controller down, remove your face from the phone! (smile)

Because I think I may be boring you right now, I want to challenge you with a question- and form it into a little learning lesson. What if it was a little person rather than a donkey I rented for my brother's bachelor party? That's correct- a midget. What if his name was Mighty Mike? What if he stood 4'3 Inches, had long sideburns, and dressed up like Elvis Presley for each event? Well, it's all true. Not one of my editors would fail to demand that I remove this fact from the book because they all believe that "dwarfism" is nothing to kid around about. We live in a time when people are very sensitive about everything, yet Mighty Mike would not be offended by my telling you this story. In fact, when I first called Mike's booking agent about hiring him, I was working for the Attorney General's office in Massachusetts in the Disability Rights division, of all places. I know- I can't make this stuff up. My focus was a project which involved improving access at Gas Stations for disabled people and small people who couldn't reach the pumps. So you might say I had become sensitized to the issues surrounding equal access to those who had some form of disability. So I was very reluctant when I dialed the number on the card to inquire about renting a small person.

I wanted to ask the booking agent a series of questions, including the proper terminology in addressing Mike. "Does he prefer to be called a small person?" I got through to Mike's booking agent and had a rather awkward conversation. In the end, Mike said to me, "Glenn, I'm a midget. You can call me a midget, or a dwarf. Call us whatever the F you want, we don't care." When I finally spoke with Mighty Mike in Vegas, he said to me, "I'm an actor available for hire. I like my work." At least at the time, he didn't seem concerned with what people thought. Here is me, Jack, and Mighty Mike, Pictured Circa 1993.

I'm not sure why today I feel like a bad person for hiring him or for telling you this story. Does my personal obligation and commitment not to demean any people include my assuming for Mighty Mike, that my hiring a small person for a party would spread a negative stereotype? Am I a lesser person for having hired Mighty Mike? Maybe. Have the "woke" police gotten to me? Are my sensitivities good or bad? I hope to answer these questions before the book is through.

Importantly, here is the deal. I'm not writing a book that judges people on whether or not they are a good person. I'm writing only to reveal sources of truth. This book is only about being a good citizen. What you do in your spare time has nothing to do with me. It's very important for my readers to understand that **I believe that the threshold for being a good person is far lower than that of being a good citizen.**

Maybe the guy who rented the midget is not qualified to be giving you advice, but some of the stuff we covered in this chapter is too important not to be said. Therefore, get outside! Climb a mountain. Bite into a lemon, swallow a goldfish, jump into a freezing cold lake (supervised). Live like my buddy "Baloose. You will be a more resilient and capable person and these are the skills we need, in order to carry out the duties of citizenship.

Now, I want to end the chapter on a light note- as if my Mighty Mike story was not light enough! (Smile)

I visited my Mom's grave on Mother's Day this year. My mom died in 2005. I realize I'm not off to a good start on the lighter note. Don't worry. It will get lighter. I arrived at her grave without any flowers and soon felt empty-handed. Anyhow, I noticed some pink flowering shrubs at the outskirts of the grounds, and so I sauntered over and started picking at them. I promise you that they were not on anyone else's grave... but they were darn close. After breaking some small limbs in the neighboring plots, I returned to my mom and placed the pink blooms and various ragweeds into the vase that flips up into place. As I was admiring my work, a woman approached from behind me, startling me at first... and said, "I noticed your clipping the shrubs." My heart sank at the thought of her witnessing my possibly illegal landscaping activities, but before my worry about her being some sort of cemetery cop overcame me... She reached out and handed me a single red rose, and said softly- "I hope you don't mind my saying hello, every mom should have a rose on Mother's Day." I learned that her name was Roberta. She had an overwhelming aura of kindness about her. She was visiting her husband and a daughter who had passed away in a tragic accident together. As we parted ways, she said in her warm voice, "It was nice speaking with you Glenn, may God bless you."

At the start of this chapter, I mentioned that faith plays a large part in my life. I choose to pray to God almost every night to give me strength. I believe faith played a role for Roberta as well. One of the things that I love most about life is how mysterious it is. Nobody can prove or deny the existence of a higher power or powers, Nor can anyone explain  how any of us even got here. This gives us the freedom to believe whatever we want about the *supernatural*[47] world. Things like divine intervention, angels, life after death, the role of fate, whether or not we have a soul, etc. Nobody can take any of my beliefs about such things away from me, particularly

---

47. supernatural: (of a manifestation or event) attributed to some force beyond scientific understanding or the laws of nature.

because they cannot disprove them. There is not a better part of life, as far as I'm concerned. I think this stuff matters- a lot. Take, for example, the Zodiac Signs (Astrological Charts) that predict personality and other things about us based only on the position of the stars at the moment of our birth (I'm a triple-fire Sagittarius, by the way) I'm in awe of how accurately it describes me. This just adds to the weirdness of it all, and I love it.

So to close this chapter, I want to ask you- How did you think Roberta became such a kind person? Maybe she Googled it- she ate right, went to the gym, and followed her doctor's prescriptive guidance. Or maybe she grew up poor and hungry and overcame those challenges to emerge self-confident and giving? Maybe for a time, like me, she grew up with every advantage but had to work her ass off to overcome her guilt. So she studied hard, played hard, and prayed a lot to emerge feeling mostly decent about herself. Maybe she made a ton of friends, traveled often to exciting places, and lived an active lifestyle. Maybe she's eaten a goldfish. Maybe she keeps her cell phone at home when she walks in the woods and when she visits her loved ones at the cemetery. Maybe she uses hope, optimism, and spirituality to lift her up when she is feeling low. And maybe she believes that a higher power is judging her actions while she is here on earth, which motivates her to be a source of good for others, doing random acts of kindness during her limited time here. Maybe she was born at a moment in time when the stars and moons in the sky were positioned just right for her to feel generally well, or maybe she just got lucky? Maybe it was a mix of all of the above. Hopefully, you get the point. We need to stop underestimating people, and this starts with ourselves. You are amazing, and 90% of the people you will meet are amazing.

Now we turn to the harder questions. If there are so many paths for people to take to being kind, tolerant, and helpful why does it seem we struggle so much? Why do our government and politics seem so *toxic*[48] and *polarizing*[49]? Why do almost half of all Americans report being sad enough at periods of their lives to seek professional help (*Major Depression*, n.d.) Why are we

---

48. toxic: very harmful or unpleasant in a pervasive or insidious way.
49. polarizing: divide or cause to divide into two sharply contrasting groups or sets of opinions or beliefs.

witnessing more terrible acts of violence against our society than ever before? What should be expected of us when it comes to solving these over-sized problems? What really matters in life? How should we be judged?

Chapter 4: The Intended Path

Those are some pretty large questions that I just posed. In order to answer them, I need to start talking about reality. There were "246 mass shootings in America in the first 155 days of 2022" (Boston Globe June 7, 2022), more than one a day. We live in times of much *perplexity*[50], yet I dedicated two of the first three chapters to talking about how great we are. I realize that all this positive information, while true, may ring a little hollow given the reality of our circumstances. I don't have to remind you of what you know all too well, that life can feel like being on a roller coaster. For all its highs, there are plenty of lows, and as wonderful as life can be, just as quickly it can take a turn. For some of us, it doesn't take much for sadness to turn into something worse. We talked about happiness too. Most of us will achieve more happiness in our lives than sadness. However, with all this talk of happiness, we know that there is a flip side of the coin. In one moment, we are standing on top of a mountain gazing at a sunset, experiencing great joy for the beauty we are seeing, and in the next moment, we feel sadness at the thought of someone we love not being with us. Even if we can get our arms around the fact that, in life, there is sadness with happiness, we seem to have bigger problems in America that we need answers for.

I have come to believe that life is all about these *contradictions* [51]. These *wildly* opposing conditions that are hard to understand and difficult to manage. I believe that having a greater understanding of these contradictions will help us greatly, not only to answer the question of how we should truly be judged but also to bond us together as Americans. This, I admit, is a large undertaking. Therefore, this chapter is broken up into sections. It starts with a quick story which I hope will be a runway for us to take flight. It's your time to fly, so strap on your seatbelt!

It starts with birds. I know what you must be thinking- I am

---

50. perplexity: a complicated or baffling situation or thing

51. contradiction: a combination of statements, ideas, or features of a situation that are opposed to one another

infatuated[52] with using animals to explain life. It's true, and I haven't even used my Ostrich yet. But I did say fly, so I think that birds fit here...

About my birds, I have a porch at my home outside of Boston (the original house dates back to early farming days, so we call it a farmers porch.) Pictured here you will see a white vase that I placed at the top of one of the interior columns, with a bird's nest next to it. Placing this vase in this location was my 23rd attempt in 23 years to stop the same birds from building a nest on my porch. Without fail, sometime in the early spring they arrive and start their construction. They are super protective of their job site. When we open the door to the porch, they fly out of the nest and head right for us, swirling over our heads as their little babies shriek. It scares the shit out of everybody, including the mailman, Doordash, Fed Ex, etc. We can't even get our deliveries anymore! Over the years, I've been placing objects in the locations where they have built-in hopes that they will someday get the point and scram. I've even climbed up the column and removed building materials as mommy and daddy bird whirl over my head in anger. Regardless of all the many things I've done to stop them, they still come. Every year, without fail. Why do I tell you about my birds?

Given the mass shootings that I just referred to, the issue of "Gun Control" was recently back in the news. As I was watching the TV, adults were trying to discuss the issues from opposite political sides but they were yelling over one another, blaming each other and not making any progress. The noise and confusion of the moment made me think about my birds, and I slipped into a daydream... (Cue the clouds and music here...)

I thought about asking a person who loves his guns, whose father

---

52. infatuated: possessed with an intense but short-lived passion or admiration for someone

and mother loved their guns, and whose grandparents loved their guns, to even begin to <u>think</u> about placing one or two new rules in our laws to make it a little harder for 18-year-olds to buy a certain type of automatic gun. At that moment, it occurred to me, it would be like me trying to have a conversation with Papa Bird. Papa Bird landed on my shoulder and I said to him, "Papa Bird, can't you see that I don't want you to build your nest on my porch? Would you please stop?" And he said, "Glenn –I see you've been making efforts to keep us off your porch. I'm sorry we keep coming each year, we truly don't even know where our desire to build on your porch comes from… However, we FEEL it very strongly and it's important to my family going back 100's of years. However, Glenn, because you've asked nicely, just for you this year we decided that we are going to drop all that. We have considered the situation more deeply, and have decided that next spring we are going to build our family nest in that big Pine tree across the street. Sorry for causing you all of the trouble, have a nice day …bye…" I had dreamt that Papa Bird would be the Bigger Bird.

Then, of course, I awoke (end clouds and music here) and returned to the actual nightmare playing out on TV. I tell this story to reinforce a basic fact about humans. We can truly be a bunch of bird brains. While that may be an attempt at being funny, the reality is that we tend to feel our way through life rather than think our way through it. This is a part of the great puzzle that has been set out before us. For example, we have the knowledge we need to prevent unhappiness in millions of people, yet we don't. We could greatly reduce mass shootings if we tried hard enough, yet we don't. We know, for example, that many healthy kids have a mentor in their lives, whether it be a parent, a coach, or a friend. We could easily set up a mentoring program in every community that would ensure that no kid would be left isolated or feel labeled as an outcast or misfit. Yet we don't. Even when there is overwhelming evidence for what we could do, we fail to do it. Why is this?

Please consider this picture. At first glance, it shows an old witch or hag, but it also reveals a young girl or princess, depending on who is looking at it. Which do you see? Two people will look at this picture and rarely see the same thing. What this picture demonstrates is that each of us attaches meaning to words, photos, and life in general in a different way. As much as we try to define greatness or happiness or try to define what is "normal" or not, we struggle because one person's definition will always be different from another. We all have different upbringings and life experiences which give us our own unique perspectives. Take, for example, when I said earlier that no man is born with evil in his heart or mind evil- that is a man-made process. Is this something we know (100%) for sure? Given who we are as people, is there really anything that we can establish as one hundred percent certain? The answer is- very little. Think about it, even if we did know something for sure, isn't it true that our fellow human beings don't want to hear about it from us? When someone talks a big game, aren't we quick to say to ourselves, "Who does this person think they are?" Especially when we're not face to face but instead behind a computer or phone, aren't we quick to call people know-it-alls or think to ourselves, "Who made them king for the day?" Even when there is *insurmountable*[53] evidence that something is true, and no matter how many people agree, doesn't it seem like there is always someone who says otherwise? This is just how things are. People make up their own reality depending on their own perspective of things and according to beliefs they hold sacred.

---

53. insurmountable: too great to be overcome

So where does this leave us? Is there any information that will cause us to figure out the many complications and confusing forces in life that we are faced with? **Are there one or two things that are so simple that even all of us Birdbrains can agree on?**

Today widespread societal peace in America eludes us, but it wasn't always this way. We have come very close in the past to solving these puzzles completely. It happened in less complex times, but it did happen. If we are able to recreate it, it can happen again.

Section One- Our Intended Path: The Enlightenment:

It started in places like Athens Greece, only a few 100 years ago, when the first schools came into being. With the discovery of language and written words, we left our primitive nature in the past. No more caveman mentalities, no more carvings in stone. "Education" allowed people to form thoughts and express themselves in a manner that would convince other people of things that were not formally agreed upon. People were figuring out what they could rely on as being true or not, and what behaviors were acceptable, or not. When we began to use paper and "pen" (a quill with ink) and printing presses for the first time it allowed the teachers in the schools to reach a wider audience. The search for knowledge and truth went into high gear and soon became known as the sciences-"the intellectual and practical activity encompassing the systematic study of the structure and behavior of the physical and natural world through observation and experiment." People began to verify their assumptions, through a process of deductive reasoning (a fancy word for thinking things through carefully without jumping to conclusions) and used evidence to support their ideas. In 1736 for example, one group of people formed an association for science research and sent an expedition across the ocean, which took months, to verify Isaac Newton's contention that the earth was round. They weren't just gonna take Newton's word for it. Scientists became known as Philosophers, also called "Philosophes" in France. I don't know why they had to come up with such fancy names for an educated person. I think it may be a French thing. These philosophes became the world's heroes, known only by single-word names, like Voltaire, Turgeou, and my favorite – Cicero! Today, it's our athletes and rappers who receive such praise. Kanye, Kobe, Lebron, Taylor, and 50 Cent!

Back then, things were very different. Back then, it was cool to grow a beard, place your hand on your chin, look to the sky, and think to oneself, "Hmmmm, this world is amazing, and there is so much I don't know about it." Back then, talking about morality and *ethics*[54] was trend-setting and all the rage. Those who were hanging out in schools, and town centers, talking about civics-*"the studies of the rights and duties of citizenship"* were admired and asked to become leaders. Philosophers became lawmakers and advisors to Kings and Emperors. It was during this period of time something amazing happened. The wisdom of those who were seeking education was appreciated by those who were less educated! Can you believe that? Well, it's true.

Then something even more amazing happened. Being nice to people and not acting like you know everything became *customary*[55]. Can you believe this? Certain courtesies- were extended to people with different opinions. Being considerate and gracious toward your fellow Americans was the *etiquette*[56] of those times. It's how you were judged. There was a right and a wrong way to speak to someone with whom you disagreed and the lines were clear. It wasn't a law, but it didn't need to be. Rather it occurred by gradual, unconscious *assimilation*[57], jumping from one person to another, by example, and enforced naturally. People who fell beneath the standards of communication were *ostracized*[58], from their friends and family, and removed from any positions of influence or power. Those who practiced humility rose up in society, whereas loudmouths and know-it-alls were shunned and kicked to the curb. Slowly this pattern repeated itself and soon enabled *prudence*[59] and

---

54. ethics: moral principles that govern a person's behavior or the conduct of an activity.

55. customary: according to the customs or usual practices associated with a particular society, place, or set of circumstances

56. etiquette: the customary code of polite behavior in society or among members of a particular profession or group.

57. assimilation: the process of taking in and fully understanding information or ideas

58. ostracized: exclude (someone) from a society or group

59. prudence: acting with or showing care and thought for the future

logic[60] to spread throughout the land, from congested city centers to far reaches of the countryside. I know how unbelievable this all sounds, but it's all true.

It was such an important time period in human civilization that we gave it a name- The Age of Enlightenment. It was also called The Age of Reason. According to Wikipedia – "Characteristics of the Age of Enlightenment" (Years 1715-1789 C.E.) "included a range of ideas centered on the value of human happiness, the pursuit of knowledge obtained by means of reason and the evidence of the senses, and ideals such as liberty, progress, toleration, *fraternity*[61]-constitutional government..." I like to use the word Education interchangeably with Enlightenment. I call this period The Age of Education, but you won't find that on Wikipedia.

The forming of America was widely regarded by philosophers all over the world as the pinnacle achievement of the Age of Enlightenment. Many believed that our founding documents, and the principles behind them, were the most advanced set of ideas ever committed to paper. In his book, "Condorcet," named after the famous French philosopher of the same name, Author Guillaume Ansart summarizes the life and work of Condorcet who helped write France's system of government. He makes it clear that the people in England and France had been working on their systems of Government for many years before America, but it was the American system that he, Condorcet deemed best. About America, Condorcet said, "America presents a country of vast dimension where several million men live whose education has preserved them from prejudice and inclined toward study and reflection. No social distinctions exist there, no rewards for ambition which could lure these men away from the natural desire to perfect their minds... and nothing there confines a part of the human race to a state of abjection where it is doomed to stupidity and misery. Therefore, there is reason to hope that a few generations from now, America, by producing almost as many men who will be busy adding to the extent of our

---

60. logic: reasoning conducted or assessed according to strict principles of validity

61. fraternity: a group of people sharing a common profession or interests

knowledge as all of Europe, will at least double its progress or make it twice as fast." (Ansart, 2015, p. 7)

At the time, fancy words such as *Tyranny*[62] and *Despotism*[63] were discussed a lot. The colonialists who were living in America as English citizens had grown tired of the British *Monarchy*[64]. The whole King and Queen thing if you will, with all of its regalia. All that, "I'm better than you because my Dad is a royal"... type of thing, the spectacular displays of superiority and all of the "*Aristocracy*[65]" stuff... had worn thin on Americans. Also, the words *ostentatious*[66] and *pretentious*[67] fit here as well. These are good words to remember- you don't ever want to be these things. Long story short, all the "British stuff" (with respect to English people today) had simply run its course. We were done. When the British Govt. in 1773, began to tax the people too much for Tea, in order to pay for a war that England had fought in Europe for their own freedom, that was the straw that broke the camel's back. Over the next few years, Americans from all differing social classes would mix together to fight this common enemy. It was through this long-lasting battle that we bonded together as one community. We were in the process of forming a shared set of uniquely American values.

Americans had learned from the many imperfections that had been revealed by trouble in other governing systems in Europe. What is most important to remember is that it was a set of values based on the premise that, in order for men to govern themselves, they must be educated. This belief became universal. It was through *virtuous*[68] leadership and the establishment of the right universal values, that we had prolonged periods of peace.

---

62. Tyranny: cruel or oppressive government or rule
63. Despotism: the exercise of absolute power especially in a cruel and oppressive way
64. Monarchy: a form of government with a monarch at the head
65. Aristocracy: as the highest class in certain societies, especially those holding hereditary titles or offices; a form of government in which power is held by the nobility
66. ostentatious: characterized by vulgar or pretentious display; designed to impress or attract notice.
67. pretentious: attempting to impress by affecting greater importance, talent, culture, etc., then is actually possessed
68. virtuous: having or showing high moral standards

Not perfection for all, of course, but peace. Nobody back then, could hold us down from reaching our goals.

Condorcet for one, thought that we were onto something BIG! Particularly, he recognized the focus and the value we were placed on the education of all people. He wrote, "Having long reflected upon the ways to improve the fate of humankind, I cannot help but think there is really only one; accelerating the progress of enlightenment. Any other means has only a passing and limited effect... Let men be enlightened, and soon you will see the good emerge effortlessly from the common will." (Ansart, 2015, p. 9) and he said, "The new nation was the first in human history to have fully recognized the natural rights of man and to have enshrined them in its founding documents... these solemn documents, which acknowledge the existence of certain fundamental, universal, and natural human rights, represented America's greatest contribution to the cause of human freedom, for they provided the best protection against **tyranny,** (there's that word) an ever-present danger..."

There were other powerful words that were written about and discussed often, during these times. *Dogmatism*[69]- *(*A weird word... makes me think about Gracie... but with important meaning)- *the tendencies of laying down principles as incontrovertibly true without consideration of evidence or the opinions of others. "* As I said earlier, people who were dogmatic, or closed-minded, did not enjoy a seat at the table for very long...and were shown the door- respectfully of course. People had manners back then. Other related ideas and types of people that were being dismissed are worth listing and defining:

1. *Fanaticism*[70]- or Fanatics- The quality of being Fanatical; filled with excessive and single-minded zeal- not accepted.
   2. *Provocateurs*[71]- a person who provokes trouble, causes dissension or the like; agitator- out of fashion, discounted.

---

69. dogmatism: the tendency to lay down principles as incontrovertibly true, without consideration of evidence or the opinions of others
70. fanatiscism: The quality of being Fanatical; filled with excessive and single minded zeal- not accepted.
71. provocateurs: a person who provokes trouble, causes dissension or the like;

54

3. Eccentrics[72]- of a person or their behavior, unconventional and slightly strange- outcasted.

4. Vanity[73]- excessive pride in one's own appearance or achievements'- not cool.

5. Conspiracist[74]- a person who supports a conspiracy theory; an explanation of an event that it claims was the result of a secret and often complex and evil plot by multiple people "- not in vogue...

6. Hardliners[75]- a member of a group, typically a political group, who adheres uncompromisingly to a set of ideas or policies "- given little attention.

Let's say you had a crazy uncle named Donny, back then, who behaved in one of these ways. You would have been proud to say to him, "Uncle D, -I don't accept your conspiracy theories. Your ideas are way too eccentric, and you offer no proof in support of your opinions... Get some civics lessons Uncle Donny and then come back and see me. Please don't let the door hit you on the way out!" (smile) We all have an "Uncle Donny", don't we? You know what he looks and acts like. I will reintroduce him later in the story.

If I were to boil down this time period, The Enlightenment, to **one message**, I believe, that the people would want us to take as their *legacy[76]* it is this; **Far more important than any government documents themselves, effective government would always require an educated citizenry.** James Madison, (1751-1836) our fourth President, who is said to be the "Father of the Constitution" said, "Knowledge will forever govern ignorance; and a people who mean to be their own governors must arm themselves with the power which knowledge gives."

---

72. eccentric: of a person or their behavior, unconventional and slightly strange- outcasted

73. vanity: excessive pride in one's own appearance or achievements

74. conspiracist: a person who supports a conspiracy theory; an explanation of an event that it claims it was the result of a secret and often complex and evil plot by multiple people

75. hardliners: a member of a group, typically a political group, who adheres uncompromisingly to a set of ideas or policies

76. legacy: the long-lasting impact of particular events, actions, etc. that took place in the past, or of a person's life

Ben Franklin himself was heard to say, "Only virtuous people are capable of freedom."(Sacks, 2020) Finally, Condorcet, in his eulogy to his good friend Mr. Franklin, to honor what the man stood for, reminded all Americans that "even under the freest of constitutions, an ignorant people is always enslaved." (Ansart, 2015, p. 18). There has never been a person who made the world a better place, than Ben Franklin. The fact that he was from Boston is only icing on the cake! He was arguably among the most gifted as a writer and inventor, but more impressive than his inventions, is the hand he had in shaping American values. These were not family values or traditional values. These were values that pertained to how to be a good citizen. Franklin led what is called a dutiful life. Nearly every day was spent *toiling*[77]- over inventions to improve mankind. About how he lived, Condorcet wrote, "had invented for himself a method by which one could hope to improve oneself by means of a small number of rules of daily observation of which was to destroy... habits of weakness, passions which are detrimental to happiness and degrade morals" (Ansart, 2015, p. 84). "He knew that thrift, regular work, and a simple life, by contributing to personal happiness, remove the interest and temptation to disturb the happiness of others and that the resulting peace to the soul makes virtues easy to practice... His system of conduct was simple, he sought to use temperance and work to ward off grief and boredom" (Ansart, p. 103) (*Siri defines *temperance*[78] *as* "abstinence from alcoholic drink; The quality of moderation or self-restraint.") I would enlarge that to mean not doing too many things that you will wake up the next day to regret. The way people lived back then is a huge part of the overall story of this book. Franklin's life and the habits and customs of those times are telling an important tale. Mr. Franklin lived a life day in and day out, without excess, and defined by the search for wisdom, understanding human excellence, and

---

77. toil: work extremely hard or incessantly

78. temperance: abstinence from alcoholic drink; The quality of moderation or self-restraint

righteousness. He taught himself how to write at the age of 12, and began to write secretly, about such things as fairness, and justice, and mistreatment of one class of person over another. (at that time, women) He snuck his letters under the door of his brother's print shop at night, so no one knew who was writing them. He wrote in a way that made complicated matters seem simple, but yet they were *eloquent*[79] and *timeless*[80]. His lessons were crafted carefully so that they could easily be digested by men of the lowest intellect, while also being appreciated by those with the highest. His publications started small but quickly grew larger in distribution. After moving to Philadelphia, he continued to write *anonymously*[81] under the nickname of Poor Richard. In time, people would come to figure out who he was and he grew a following. This following would grow and grow.

"He formed a club among those of the inhabitants of Philadelphia whose station in life was close to his. It consisted of only twelve people, and their number never increased. However, prompted by his advice, most members soon set up other similar associations. This way he made sure that (the clubs) would be animated by the same spirit."(Ansart, 2015, p. 81)

The Rules of Ben Franklin's Clubs:

- **To declare not to harbor any feeling of animosity against any club member.**
- **To profess an equal affection for all men, whatever their creed.**
- **To regard as an act of tyranny (there's that word again) any infringement upon freedom of worship or opinion.**
- **To love truth for itself, to try to know it, to take pleasure in hearing it, to strive to spread it."**

In fact, there was a fine levied upon people who violated the rules of engagement. "In Franklin's club in Philadelphia, one would pay a fine whenever one indulged in harsh words. The

---

79. eloquent: fluent or persuasive in speaking or writing
80. timeless: not affected by the passage of time or changes in fashion
81. anonymous: (of a person) not identified by name; of unknown name

men most *intrepid*[82] in their self-assurance were <u>forced to use expressions of doubt</u> and to grow accustomed in their speech to a <u>modesty</u> which...would procure to the benefit of not hurting the feelings of others... "(Ansart, 2015, p. 83)

Mr. Franklin would go on to build a library, several schools, and a hospital in his hometown of Philadelphia, but not many people would realize that he was behind them. He never dropped even a hint of his accomplishments. "One would look in vain for a line he could be suspected of having written for his own glory"(Ansart, 2015, p. 104). "When he would put forth a project for an institution, he would carefully avoid claiming the idea for himself."(Ansart, 2015, p. 84) "His discoveries on electricity, which assure him everlasting fame, are contained in a few letters to his friends."(Ansart, 2015, p. 103).

On the day of the signing of the US Constitution, which he helped write, Mr. Franklin said; "Mr. President, I confess that there are several parts of this constitution which I do not approve, but I am not sure that I shall never approve them. For having lived long, I have experienced many instances of being obliged by better information, or fuller consideration, to change opinions even on important subjects, which I once thought right, but found to be otherwise... I doubt too whether any other convention we can obtain may be able to make a better constitution... It therefore astonishes me, Sir, to find this system approaching so near to perfection as it does; and I think it will astonish our enemies... Thus I consent, Sir, to this constitution because I expect no better, and because I am not sure it is not the best. (The American Presidency p. 28). Mr. Franklin's sense of modesty is a most superb example of someone we need to *exemplify*[83]. The historical texts make clear that most people during these times shared similar values. Americans showed great optimism for the spirit and capabilities of their fellow man. I could bury you with quotations from the likes of George Washington, Thomas Jefferson, James Madison, Alexander Hamilton, and others from the time that demonstrate that their intentions and motivations were "pure." I hope that you will find your way to bury yourself with readings about the people who shaped the forming of our national government. What you will

---

82. Intrepid: fearless, adventurous (often used for humorous effect)
83. exemplify: be a typical example of

find is that although not perfect (no men are), **they developed character in a time when doing so was the ultimate shared goal in our culture!**

Our founders, and the men and women of the time had high *ambitions*[84] that they could figure out all that was most important for them to know-_However, most importantly they knew that they couldn't figure out everything. It was by and through this process of collective reasoning and shared modesty, that they came to realize something very important- **that the process of how we arrive at the truth is more important than the truth itself.** Therefore, **they placed an overwhelming amount of effort into communicating effectively with each other.** If you take nothing else from this book- only take that. In 18th century America people placed respecting each other on the top of the priority list. This started with assuming that, "everyone you will ever meet knows something that you don't" (Bill Nye). That someone with whom you disagreed, still had good intentions and had something worth your learning.

During these few years, we figured out the conditions under which peace occurs. A code of conduct, befitting an American citizen, was formed. It began in private associations and moved with great speed to the public sphere. The attitudes, and beliefs about how to communicate became our *customs*[85]. Not by law or by force, but rather through effective leadership, we successfully created an American communication code that ensured a mutual respect of each other. It was this shared belief system and a trust in each other that we created a governmental system that has been more effective than any other ever known by mankind. The Articles of Confederation were written in 1776. It would take another 11 years to establish a federal government which was acceptable to the people of the various states. I have come to learn just how astonishing the work and the result; given the challenge involved.

I also believe that in order for us to have a working country that you can feel safe in, and feel proud about, we will have to return

---

84. ambitions: a strong desire to do or to achieve something, typically requiring determination and hard work
85. customs: the official department that administers and collects the duties levied by a government on imported goods.

to adoption of the core principles which guided the Founders in the forming of the United States of America.

Before moving ahead, it's very important that I clarify something. It's about the allowance of slavery by the same people who I have just written so positively about. Slavery is one of the largest mistakes ever made by mankind, incomparable in its scope. It also ranks close to the most confusing contradictions that there ever was. (There is only one larger. I end the chapter with it). It was a slave owner himself, (Thomas Jefferson) who wrote our Declaration of Independence, stating that, "All men are created equal..." How could he, and other white men who signed our Constitution, set forth in writing, that all men would be treated with equal opportunity regardless of skin color, but then act so differently? The mistreatment of black, native American and non-white people over the course of our country's history is a stain on our country. As we work through its continuing impact on the lives of people today, what I would ask, respectfully to those who were mistreated is this: Please do not let our history of injustice define who we are as people, and who we can be moving forward. I ask everyone, first to never deny the disparate impact that slavery has had on people of color. I also ask with the utmost respect that the victims of our cruelty, to not let what happened long ago, or a single document itself, get in the way of our restoring our belief in each other. The "Framers" (people who drafted our Constitution) were not perfect people we know. They knew the documents which established our *democracy*[86]-, were only ink on pieces of paper and were as imperfect as human beings themselves. This would include interpretations of the laws that allowed for slavery. We will forever need to rely on each other to make a government by the people, for the people, work as intended and ultimately this will require that we believe there is mostly good in people. Many Framers of our Constitution voted against the practice but tragically the *abolitionists-*[87]" in the north surrendered to the greedy landowners of the south who profited greatly from slave labor. The battle would rage on for years, and (as you realize) is

---

86. democracy: a system of government by the whole population or all the eligible members of a state, typically through elected representatives.

87. abolitionists: a person who favors the abolition of a practice or institution.

still raging. I say nothing here, which forgives their ultimate choices. As you know slavery would be abolished, by law on December 18, 1865.

In closing this section, our laws were meant to be changeable, decided by good people, of all colors and races, (and regardless of our differences) today and moving forward. Like so many things in life, we are best served to proceed with a balanced approach. As much as we (the *posterity*[88] of white American birdbrains) cannot forget slavery and act accordingly to right the wrongs of the past, we (the posterity of Non-White, Black, and Brown American birdbrains) must also- in equal measure I respectfully suggest, find it within yourself to recognize people when they are making efforts to ensure we never forget, to think about possible forgiveness, and act accordingly. Reestablishment of the values spoken about in this section is our only chance of ever coming to terms with each other.

Section Two- Our Intended Path: Moderation

Siri defines *moderation*[89] as, *the avoidance of excess or extremes; especially in one's behaviors or political opinions.* This may sound boring to you, but this section will be anything but boring. I have a lot to say about moderation. I am going to try to make the case for moderation in a very unique way. In fact, I am going to disturb my own comfort level and maybe yours too.

Today, too many people hate each other without even knowing one another. We avoid people because we don't want to talk to them about stuff. Many good people are afraid to say anything or run for politics. People are leaving careers as teachers because they've been threatened. In her Ted Talk, Ms. Celeste Headlee cited a survey of over 10,000 people, who said that we are more divided as Americans than ever before. (TEDx Talks, 2016) We've spent too many years like this. We could sit back and just hope that people are so tired of it all, that it would cause us to change. However, I fear that our tiredness alone will not get it done. We need something BIG! We need someone to say

---

88. posterity: all future generations of people

89. moderation: the avoidance of excess or extremes; especially in one's behaviors or political opinions

something or do something differently that will cause us to turn things around. We all want change to come. This section is my best effort.

I want to start with a metaphor, but don't worry, it doesn't have any animals in it. This time we are a lifeboat in a storm-tossed ocean, we have lost the safety and security of our mothership. Millions of us adrift at sea lost and losing hope. We have set our mothership on fire because we argued to the point of its destruction. Now appears a single lifeboat! Enemies clinging to its opposing sides. We are left with only one choice, to reach upward across the raft, grab hands and pull to the middle. The middle is the only place where the raft balances. Please think hard about that. **The fact that a shared raft will not float unless people move closer to one another and meet in the MIDDLE is only ONE example of many that should prove to us the importance of seeking the center.**

I've come to believe that we've been missing something... Big. Really BIG. I think moderation and seeking the center, between two opposing extremes, is not only important, I think that God (or some higher and unknown power) has been sending us clues about the importance of moderation for a long time, and for some reason, we are just not listening. I worry that my mentioning GOD too much in this book will turn some people off. I learned at a young age that we need to be careful if, when, and how we call in the name of God. In fact, I remember clearly the first time I learned this. I was a freshman in high school running the mile test in gym class. It was a hot day, in early September on the outdoor track. After crossing the finish line, I fell to the ground and uttered the words, "God Damn." Coach Foley, who everyone called Foles- a legend in our small town, called me over... "Brother Cort" (Foles called everyone brother or sister for their first name followed by last name- adding to his legendary status) he said, "I never want to hear you using the lord's name in vain." I didn't know what it meant to take someone's name in vain. I think he meant carelessly or without serious application to some meaning but I never did again and I am not going to start now. Talking about God should be serious business. It's not something to be taken lightly- I leave it to you to wonder why. But I've been thinking a lot about this, and I just have no other way to say it -Moderation must be God's will for us, there is just too much evidence of it.

As I've gotten older, and witnessed things in our society most recently that I never thought I would see in my lifetime, I have come to believe more strongly that it's God's puzzle we are solving for. In fact, I'm gonna take this a step further. I think each of us carries a little higher power within ourselves. We are each connected to God's purpose and we each carry a part of him (or her) with us. We need to follow his clues and carry out his intentions in order to make things work down here on Earth- it's a matter of our survival.

Have I become so desperate that I would stoop so low, to call God into this, unless I truly believed he had a plan for us? While admitting to some desperation, I would never do that. I would never talk about God in a *frivolous*[90] manner. Therefore, I want to offer some proof that there is a plan and we are all connected to it, and that moderation is a big part of it. You can then decide for yourself if I am reaching too far. Take these words- "GOD Grant me the serenity to accept those things that I cannot change, the courage to change the things that I can, and the wisdom to know the difference? "Who gave us these words? A human yes? How about these words, "Do unto others only that you would have done unto yourself?" Take these words, "the spirit of liberty is the spirit which is not too sure that it is right, it is the spirit which seeks to understand the mind of other men and women which weighs their interest alongside its own without bias." *(*Chief Judge Learned Hand). When I read such words from people, it's hard for me not to think that in part, they are speaking the words of GOD. It's not that much of a stretch, is it?

In earlier times people were not afraid of making these connections known. In fact, just a few years ago organized religion was a much bigger deal than it is today. In the last few years, our society has had a large move away from organized religion. Could our general move away from religion be in part a cause of our problems today- sure I do think it's part of it, but without getting too far into that, I want to continue to make the case for God's plan. Did I just say that? A simple human being like me, trying to tell you about God's plan ? Let me restate this: I want to offer certain clues about moderation that prove that there is an intended path for us. Before you think I'm nuts (for

90. frivolous: not having any serious purpose or value.

the second or third time?), please consider all these clues carefully before reaching any conclusions. Here are a just few of the strongest clues that have convinced me that our intended path is one of moderation:

Clue number 1 is the Biggie- The Narcissist and the Super Empath

The most compelling clue of all for seeking the MIDDLE has to do with self-confidence. What would you rather have too much or too little? If you display too much, people won't like you because you come across as a know-it-all, selfish and *overbearing*[91]. You make the world a more unpleasant place for everyone around you, but because you are so concerned with yourself- you don't realize it. Therefore, over time you will lose all your friends, and die alone- Sorry. I just briefly described a *narcissist.*[92]

The opposite of having too much self-confidence is having too little. This personality type is called a "Super Empath." These people are among the nicest people you've ever met. They display almost endless kindness for everyone they meet. They make the world a better place to be for everyone around them, however, because they prioritize the feelings of others they tend to shortchange themselves. Empaths often feel insecure around other people who come off as more confident. Over time they can develop social anxiety and a fear of other people, so they avoid people altogether. Many die having been misunderstood as antisocial or introverted and fall well short from living their fullest life. Over time they too lose friends and tend to die alone- Sorry.

I'm not a doctor, as you might have already figured out. I'm being dramatic here to make my point. That is why I've placed the more *clinical*[93] description of these conditions on an Exhibit.

These personality traits exist on a scale from not serious at all, to

---

91. overbearing: unpleasantly or arrogantly domineering.
92. narcissist: a person who has an excessive interest or admiration in themselves
93. clinical: relating to the observation and treatment of actual patients rather than theoretical or laboratory studie

very serious, but many of you are becoming one or the other as I type. The great majority of people, with these two opposing conditions, without treatment, are less happy than their wonderful selves can be. It's sad to see- on both sides of the spectrum, and it's been hard for me to watch these two different types of people not get along because they are not aware.

Some narcissistic tendencies in a moderate form are good for us. In fact, many young people with narcissistic tendencies are great salespeople because they spend their early careers needing to prove their worth. They often hide the more *repulsive*[94] features of their personality type for years. You may not see it yet, but when it gets bad, someone who is becoming a real narcissist, is someone who you can't get away from fast enough. They are always needing to get in the last word, thinking that their opinion must be the only one that matters. They are always talking about themselves and often dropping hints of their own accomplishments. Is this you already? I hope not. A current friend, maybe? Not for long. There is nothing about a narcissist that makes you smile or that would impress you. So be careful. You don't want to become one of these people. I've never met a narcissist that I could tell you a funny story about. Narcissists just want to make you puke.

The super empath is just the opposite. Super Empaths make many friends early in life because they are people pleasers, but as they grow up, a hole in their own self-image opens up, which leads to problems. Many fill up this hole by drinking or using drugs. They make everyone around them feel great all the time, but sadly they don't feel as good as they should about themselves. Is this you?

There are a million worthwhile stories to tell about empaths. I want to tell you a quick story about one special super-empath in my life, my wife Brooke. (Brooke has approved of my writing about her in this way). One time while out to dinner our waiter offered us three extra jumbo shrimp for half the price if we ordered the standard shrimp cocktail appetizer. I felt like a few shrimp to start but was more fired up for my steak and cheesecake which would soon follow, so I ordered the standard and said "No thanks; for the added shrimp." My wife interjected

---

94. repulsive: arousing intense distaste or disgust.

and said, "Oh no-we will take the extra shrimp." After wolfing down my shrimp and ordering my main meal I noticed that there were three shrimp still on the table and that Brooke had not eaten any. I asked if something was wrong, or if she felt ok, lost her appetite, or something. She said, "Oh no, I just felt bad for him, (The Waiter!) I think he may have wanted us to get the extra shrimp." We laughed at her cuteness, as we do so many times. As if the waiter could care less if we had ordered his extra shrimp.

Sometimes we laugh together about how she responds to Text messages. "Lorna didn't return my text (which she sent five seconds earlier...) is she mad at me?" "Did I say the right thing just then?" When the "narcissistic texter" is just the opposite. Texting looks like this "I texted Lorna (five seconds ago) and she didn't respond yet. Who does she think she is! The hell with her, I deserve better than this."

Wouldn't you know that treatment for narcissism involves re-learning skills which the super empath has and treatment for the super empath is re-learning skills which the narcissist has. People with thicker skin need to work harder at seeing how they may come across to others. While people with thinner skin need to work harder at seeing how they may be overreacting. I am not trying to define what normal is here. Our self-image is always changing and fluctuating. There are degrees of normalcy in this regard. Not one of us has the perfect amount of self-confidence at all times... What I am saying is that if there were a perfect amount of self-confidence, it would be right in the middle of the two opposite extremes.

As with so many other things in life, the closest we can come to perfection is most often found in the middle. Millions of people in our country suffer from these conditions, and in their most extreme forms, they are wreaking havoc on their families and our society at large. Super empaths tend to get walked on by narcissists. The narcissistic personality type is widespread in America and this is doing a whole lot more damage to our society than we are currently accounting for.

Mayo Clinic's definition of Narcissism is one of several types of personality disorders is a mental condition in which people have an inflated sense of their own importance, a deep need for excessive attention and admiration, troubled relationships, and a lack of empathy for others. But behind this mask of extreme confidence lies a fragile self-esteem that's vulnerable to the slightest criticism. People with narcissistic personality disorder may be generally unhappy and disappointed when they're not given the special favors or admiration they believe they deserve. They may find their relationships unfulfilling, and others may not enjoy being around them. People with the disorder can:

- Have an exaggerated sense of self-importance.
- Have a sense of entitlement and require constant, excessive admiration.
- Expect to be recognized as superior even without achievements that warrant it.
- Exaggerate achievements and talents.
- Be preoccupied with fantasies about success, power, brilliance, beauty or the perfect mate
- . Believe they are superior and can only associate with equally special people.
- Monopolize conversations and belittle or look down on people they perceive as inferior.
- Expect special favors and unquestioning compliance with their expectations.
- Take advantage of others to get what they want.
- Have an inability or unwillingness to recognize the needs and feelings of others.
- Be envious of others and believe others envy them.
- Behave in an arrogant or haughty manner, coming across as conceited, boastful and pretentious
- .Insist on having the best of everything — for instance, the best car or office.

At the same time, people with narcissistic personality disorder have trouble handling anything they perceive as criticism, and they can:

- Become impatient or angry when they don't receive special treatment.
- Have significant interpersonal problems and easily feel slighted
- React with rage or contempt and try to belittle the other person to make themselves appear superior,
- Have difficulty regulating emotions and behavior,
- Experience major problems dealing with stress and adapting to change,
- Feel depressed and moody because they fall short of perfection,
- Have secret feelings of insecurity, shame, vulnerability and humiliation.

People with narcissistic personality disorder may not want to think that anything could be wrong, so they may be unlikely to seek treatment. If they do seek treatment, it's more likely to be for symptoms of depression, drug or alcohol use, or another mental health problem. But perceived insults to self-esteem may make it difficult to accept and follow through with treatment. A narcissistic personality disorder causes problems in many areas of life, such as relationships, work, school or financial affairs. Treatment for personality disorders centers around talk therapy (psychotherapy). If you're feeling overwhelmed by sadness, or feeling any of the above traits in the extremes, Getting the right treatment can help make your life more rewarding and enjoyable".

Now, to other clues for moderation:

Clue 2- Nature v. Nurture. Over hundreds of years, caring and smart people have debated what causes us to have the personalities that we do. Some doctors believe that we are more influenced by our nature- our "genes" and stuff which is baked into us prior to our birth. There is another camp residing on the opposing side, that believes it is more our life experiences after birth and our upbringing (our nurture) that will determine who we are. Well- I've searched long and hard for scientific proof that one is more impactful than another, and guess what, centuries worth of debate and study, and there is no conclusive evidence anywhere! Wouldn't you know? They both matter- in roughly equal measurements!

Clue 3- For over 3500 years, in Chinese Culture, it is widely believed that all forces of life consist of two parts. The symbol for Yin and Yang is pictured here representing "interconnected opposite forces" "The yin-yang (ie. Taijitu symbol) shows a balance between two opposites with a portion of the opposite element in each... Many natural dualities (such as light and dark, fire and water, expanding and contracting) are thought of as physical manifestations of the duality of life. All things come together and find energy in their opposite. "Yin is characterized as slow, soft... femininity... and night time. Yang, by contrast, is fast, hard... masculinity, and daytime." (*Yinyang (Yin-yang)* | *Internet Encyclopedia of Philosophy*, n.d.) According to their beliefs (and I'm summarizing greatly here) there is an energy chamber located at our center point, called the Dantian that resides within us. When our breath enters and leaves this chamber with the proper rhythm and concentration of mind, it balances our body with our mind and brings us optimum health. (Quinn, 2020) You may have heard of the martial arts, Yoga, or TAI CHI, or of the benefits of meditation- it's ultimately all about finding balance in our lives. These concepts only date back 3500 years. I wonder what we should do with this information. Maybe we should ignore it? Let's move on to Clue 4.

4- *CryoTherapy[95]*. Doctors say that if we go from extreme hot (sauna or jacuzzi) to extreme cold (icy water plunge, or freezing cold ocean swim) that it is great for our health. I once did the "Turkey Plunge", which is a Thanksgiving morning dive into the ocean in Nantucket and I almost croaked. I cannot report that it felt good for me. But the science is clear.

5- We are told to eat a balanced meal, consisting of equal parts protein, (fish, meat, eggs, chicken) starch (potatoes, rice, etc)

---

95. cryotherapy: the use of extreme cold in surgery or other medical treatment

dairy (milk), and fruits and vegetables. Doing so, the science says, makes us live healthier and longer lives.

6. We have an equator that divides the earth between north and south directly in the middle. I wonder why?

7. Doctors tell us that we each have an *equilibrium*[96]*-a state of balance or a stable situation where opposing forces cancel each other out and where no changes are occuring...* I wonder why?

8. We aim a dart or arrow in the middle of a target when playing darts or archery to win the game.

9. We stay in the middle of our lane when driving a car, or else we crash and maybe die.

10. The balance beam was the first sport in the Olympics (I'm not sure if this is true but it sounds good).

11. Do you want the water in the shower too hot or too cold?

12. Frizzy hair or oily hair? Which one do you want?

Last but certainly not least, I give you lucky clue number 13! Think about the physical construction of our bodies themselves. Directly in the middle of our bodies is the man's penis... (why is that word so hard to write? Haha) and a woman's vagina.. (just no easy way to write these words...) Now let me ask you- is there a more middle point in our bodies, than these two locations? Of course not. Now, what happens when these center most spots meet up? The miracle of producing life itself! You may call this *"coincidence"*- but I believe it speaks for itself. I hope this is a "drop the mic" moment... for me. Honestly, can I make this shit up?

I wonder if I'm reaching just a little bit here. Let me think about this for a second...Am I reaching? No- I am not. Think about it, what would you like to be, too dependent or too independent? Too emotional or not emotional enough? Too charismatic or not charismatic enough? Should we have total trust in something or someone or no trust at all? Too much cheesecake for dessert or none? Seriously, if some can be so strong, and some can be so weak, if some can be so right and others so wrong if some can be so happy and some so sad... isn't there too much evidence that someone is trying to tell us something? GO TO THE MIDDLE!- CHOOSE THE MIDDLE!- THE MIDDLE IS WHERE WE

---

96. equilibrium: a state of balance or a stable situation where opposing forces cancel each other out and where no changes are occuring

BELONG!

Too much government or too little government? Too much regulation and control or too little regulation and control? Should we have too much fear of the government? Or too much reliance on the government? Hint- The correct amount is in the middle of two opposing extremes. Great American and 36th President of the US Dwight Eisenhower spoke of finding the middle ground in our politics when he said, we need to "balance between the private economy and the public economy... balance between our essential requirements as a nation and the duties imposed by the nation on the individual... Good judgment seeks balance and progress; lack of it eventually finds imbalance and frustration."(Brooks, 2015, p. 72)

I've spent enough time calling us birdbrains for you to understand that another big key to our success is to greatly limit what we ask of people. By asking our fellow citizens to meet in the middle when it comes only to dealing with politics, we don't ask too much. Americans are very passionate about our individual freedoms. We don't want to be told what to do. We need to let people do whatever they want in their personal lives. This is worth repeating. We shouldn't spend our time trying to define what is normal when it comes to what people do in their personal lives. But can we at least agree that there is normal as it relates to being a citizen? Can we isolate our judgment of other people, ONLY to what it means to be a citizen? I believe we must. I am very optimistic, as were the Framers of the Constitution, that we can narrowly define the duties and obligations that we owe each other as citizens. Just as people have accepted that they need to register a car or pay taxes to the local government to plow the roads and build bridges across rivers, we can make the requirements of being a good citizen very easy to follow, and enforce. **We can only know a few things for sure in life- We need to add to this short list "what it means to be a good citizen."**

C. Everett Koop, Former US Surgeon General (1916-1938) reminds us that we do not need to agree on everything, and we don't all need to be best friends. When he said, "The American ideal is not that we all agree with each other, or even that we like each other. It is that we will respect each other's rights, especially the right to be different. And that, at the end of the day, we will understand that we are one people, one country, and one community and that our well-being is inextricably bound up with the well-being of each and every one of our fellow citizens." C. Everett Koop was a moderate. All bigger people are political moderates. Moderates fight to the end for things that we hold sacred, but by sprinkling in a little modesty, we do it in a way that is more likely to cause the other side to come along with us.

We all don't need to believe the same things. There is plenty of room for disagreement... and even strong dislike. This should never change. But there needs to be some code of conduct befitting an American citizen, or for any citizen for that matter who lives in a shared society. To be radical in your political positions, yelling over people, is wrong. To place yourself in the shoes of your political opponent, and to find compromise is right. Being a good citizen requires balancing your own needs, with the needs of others. Having a conversation with someone with whom you disagree requires equal parts talking and listening. Agreement among human beings is found when two people undertake a process of give and take – in equal measurements.

Americans spend billions of dollars a year to keep our hair balanced, but do you know how much we spend on teaching kids how to maintain patience when confronted by a classmate they disagree with? Zero. We can do better than this. To choose compromise does not mean that you need to hand over your freedoms to other people. For readers who may worry that I want to steal your freedoms, in fact, I want to do the opposite. I want to unleash our freedom.

I want to review the takeaways from The Intended Path- in six easy steps:

1. Only an educated and enlightened person can build a sense of modesty which is strong enough to overcome the negative tendencies of the human mind.
2. Modesty is a learned virtue that comes about through observance of certain daily routines, requiring self-sacrifice.
3. Only a person who develops, and maintains, a sense of modesty can practice moderation.
4. Moderation is the key to managing the two opposing sides of

life's many contradictions.

5. Self-governance (by the people for the people) presents complications that can only be solved with a moderate approach.

6. There is ONLY normal when it comes to acting like a citizen.

Was that BIG enough for you?!

Chapter 5: The Path, Grande Finale

I may be breaking some rules here, but I think that my conclusion of the Intended Path is so important that it deserves its own Chapter. I'm wondering whether you think that by being a rule breaker, I am more of a Republican or Democrat? But that's for later. Right now, I cannot wait to give you the Grande Finale.

I feel like I need a drum roll here given the significance of these next few words! I've kept Dale Carnegie's book by my bedside for a number of years. (Cole & Carnegie, 2012)

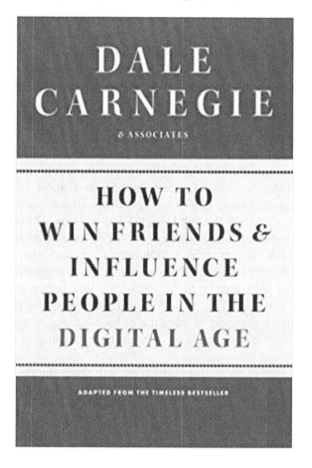

Please think about these words:

"Every man is entitled to be valued for his best moments. Think about that for a moment. Which relationship is most strained in your life right now? What would it look like if you began focusing on that person's best moments and sought to affirm them? This doesn't presuppose the person doesn't have his faults. It doesn't even presume he has fewer faults than fine qualities. He might be a broken man with years of waste and wrongdoing in his wake. But one thing you can be sure of: if you aim to influence him to change, repeatedly pointing out his rap sheet will do you little good. If instead you begin to remind him of what he could be- not with hypothetical hype, but with his own history of goodness, of success, of insight, even if only a brief history – something inside him would have cause to awaken. He could begin to see what he still can be, despite what he has been. When we treat man as he is, we make him worse than he is; when we treat him as if he already were what he potentially could be, we make him what he should be."

These are the most impactful words I've ever read. What do you think the world would look like, if we all lived by these words? Well, what if I said that I think these words and our living by them, are the very basis of human survival and evolution? You might think I was crazy right -for the fourth time...? Please hear me out. At the outset of chapter four, I mentioned the importance of managing a few of life's largest and most confusing contradictions: Emerson's words reveal the largest contradiction of all. Numero Uno, the Big Dog, the Big Kahuna. There is none bigger. A better understanding of this contradiction is the breakthrough society needs. The great contradiction is this (Drum Roll please)... The traits which we need according to our predestined path, are the most difficult for us to maintain. That's it! Were you expecting more? If you are disappointed in me, please grab a popsicle or something, because our planet's very future existence may be riding on your understanding of this.

The truth is, that for reasons which we will never understand, the unknown forces of our universe, (or God whichever you may wish to believe) make self-sacrifice and related virtues of temperance, and *forbearance*[97] of another man's faults, one of our smallest muscles, and the hardest one to keep strong particularly as we age. Emerson knew, in stating the words above, that the **people who need our love and compassion most, often are those who deserve it least.** Doing the opposite of our instincts, and understanding the *counterintuitive*[98] truths about life are the key to our success. I know how crazy this sounds, and what a bummer it may be to hear, but please bear with me. What has been proven to be true over hundreds of years, established by old (religion and philosophy) and new sources of truth, (modern science) is that each time we resist the *perversities*[99] that exist in our nature we are rewarded. Think about the feeling you get after helping a neighbor, visiting an elderly grandparent, or completing a hard task. You get this warm feeling, like the "runners high" after finishing a race. Of all the other feelings that I may discuss in this book, this one rules. While all others are temporary this one is permanent.

You may have heard about a super triathlete by the name of David Goggins. He is the guy who broke the world record for pull-ups by doing 4030 of them in 17 hours. His advice for us is that each time we push ourselves beyond the point we think we could, we reach a higher mental threshold for resilience. He introduces voluntary hardships and extreme physical challenges into his life often, to satisfy his thirst for human excellence. He teaches that the more we can endure physical pain, and or at least recognize life as some type of daily endurance test… the stronger our ability to cope with stress and stay mentally well. Basically, the discomfort we feel when working out today, is less discomfort we feel tomorrow. His books are bestsellers. As of my last check, he had 5.8 Million followers on Instagram.

Socrates and his student Aristotle placed the concept of doing less for yourself and more for others, into hyperdrive. They say that serving others, and enduring sacrifice, is the only way to achieve true happiness. Socrates said, "The just man is one who does good by his friend certainly, but also does good to those

---

97. forbearance: patient self-control; restraint and tolerance.
98. counterintuitive: contrary to intuition or to common-sense expectation (but often nevertheless true).
99. perversity: a deliberate desire to behave in an unreasonable or unacceptable way; contrariness

who have harmed him, thereby seeking to convert an enemy into a friend. It is never right to right a wrong with a wrong, or when we suffer evil to defend ourselves by doing evil in return." (Plato & Fowler, 1947, p. 173) I believe this to be true, however, I also believe they ask a lot of us. We don't need everyone to be as cool as these guys. Take the concept of forgiveness, I find it close to impossible, yet most of the religions of the world would tell us that God would want us to fully forgive those who harm us. That would require an effort that I am unsure that I have in me. I've heard people say "what doesn't kill us makes us stronger." and that pain is weakness leaving the body. These statements may be true, but I believe it's not about making yourself miserable all day long or feeding the chickens all day long, or doing 4,000 pushups in 19 hours...I believe it's more about balance than anything else. I think it's enough that we get to the **middle.**

In earlier times we had a breakthrough. Through great leadership and an unwavering belief in the good of the human spirit, we found our way to trusting each other and establishing a widely held set of values. **Whether or not you believe that by living a certain way, by being modest and moderate, Ben Franklin and people like him were doing the work of God is up to you, but I hope you do. Because now more than ever, we need it.**

People have definitely moved away from modesty and moderation. Through poor leadership, our shared sense of history and trust in one another is slipping away. We've come well off the intended path. Fortunately, my theory on how we got to our new place is fairly straightforward. In the last few years, we've been asking too much of each other, and we've had too much change too quickly. The way of the new world, with all the wires, the cloud, satellites, drones and the constant digital communications is drowning us. It's way too much, way too fast. We just can't handle all the changes- You know, the whole elephant and birdbrain thing...

We've in essence scattered the pieces of the puzzle all over the table. Like a doctor who needs to identify a cancerous tumor very clearly before removing it, we can only be successful in eliminating our problems by understanding the root causes. So now we will turn our attention to how we have lost our way. This will include what I call the rise of the Bucking Broncos, which culminated in a massive storm of sorts and created our new normal. With a greater understanding of how we got to our new place, I am confident that we can find the pieces of the puzzle and put it (and us) back together again.

Chapter 6: The Rise of the Bucking Broncos

I must say, I finished up the last chapter with some really boring stuff. Live your life according to old-fashioned values, like Ben Franklin did- **BORING!** Be modest and moderate-**BORING.** Grow up being mindful of the duties and obligations of citizenship -**SUPER BORING!** I'm sorry. I feel like I've let you down. If there's one thing I despise... It's boring. I feel like misbehaving right now! The temptation to be bad is so strong. It feels good to act out, even to be mean. My mother used to say to me, "An idle mind is the devil's workshop." True Mom, I know that- **BORING!** My Dad used to say to me, "Stay busy son- the harder you work the luckier you get." Thank you, Dad. That sounds like great advice -**BORING!**

Here it is kids, then I am done with this boring stuff. Our ability to commit to the intended path, my "Chapter Four Stuff" is boring as hell. In fact, I have come to believe that our desire to do the wrong thing, rather than the right thing, is our default mode. I'm a closet adrenaline junkie. I hate self-control more than anyone. I feel my energy wander from doing the right thing to the wrong more often than I would like to admit. I have a strong hunch that most people who are in prison right now understand what I'm talking about.

Think about it. It's only after people have acted out in such a way to have been placed behind bars, or otherwise destroyed their lives, when they realize that what they needed was a little more Ben Franklin in their lives... I am quite confident that they would tell us, "If I could have only learned at a young age about how to control my emotions, I wouldn't be here." They would also tell us how they lost their freedom because they chased their freedoms, <u>without limitation</u>. There were over 2000 people, who called themselves "Freedom Fighters" and many were arrested and jailed for their role in the demonstration that turned violent at our Nation's Capital on Jan 6th, 2021. The Freedom Fighters followed their instincts, and by doing so, got exactly the opposite of what they wanted. The truth is that people who say "follow your instincts" are dead wrong. If you follow your instincts without limitation, you are likely to wind up in prison.

However, the reality of being human makes it hard for us to avoid acting on pure emotion or avoiding temptation. The reality of life makes it easy for us to deviate from the *righteous*[100] path, even when we are crystal clear on what that path looks like. We are a vulnerable species, and for many of us, the duties and responsibilities of citizenship, and life in general, are simply too much to handle.

In the beginning of Chapter four, I promised you an Ostrich. Well here he is- pictured with his head in the sand.

Mr. Ostrich represents those in society today who have lost their way, who have come off the intended path. Mr. Ostrich falls into one or more of the following pissed off, and sick and tired of it all   categories:

    1. tired of all the emails, texts and digital messages bombarding us daily;

    2. tired of hearing from others about which type of people are underserved, or disadvantaged (when most of us have a pretty solid radar for that type of thing)

    3. Sick and tired of not being listened to

    4. being denied opportunity by those who seemingly have more power, and better lives.

---

100. righteous: (of a person or conduct) morally right or justifiable; virtuous

Many of us could fall into some of these categories as well, but what separates Mr. Ostrich, is that he has placed his head in the sand- he is not listening to any alternative viewpoints anymore. Sadly most ostriches also fall into two other camps. Most have grown to believe that the government sucks, and or
that life has become so confusing that it's not worth caring anymore. This is of course the worst category of all, particularly for those of us who still care.

I have reason to believe that you, my reader, have not become an Ostrich yet... but that you do know what one looks like. In the last chapter I introduced "Uncle Donny" as an imaginary character, and I assumed that you, like me, might have at least one in your family. Uncle Donny or maybe in your case, your crazy Aunt Delores is your classic "Ostrich." He (or she) has grown to be the opposite of modest and moderate. Uncle Donny would tell Ben Franklin to kiss his ass! Uncle Donny knows what he knows, and what he doesn't know is your problem. Everyone knows when Uncle D arrives at the Thanksgiving dinner. He is the most entertaining fella but typically *crass*[101] in his demeanor. Hearing people out, and discussing political issues calmly is not his thing. To make matters worse, in most cases, he's proud of it. The proud Ostrich (who represents a large percentage of the Ostrich family) thinks that the rest of us have lost our minds, so he wears his disgust for you and me as a badge of honor. When the ostrich puts his ear muffs on today, he does so in your face because he thinks that he is drowning out a *mortal enemy*[102]. He and other Ostriches create *emblems*[103]- such as flags, hats, and vests, which they wear with great pride to remind everyone of where they stand. When it gets to this stage, you are either with him or against him. It's important to keep in mind that we have proud ostriches on both sides of our current political divide.

I have plotted Mr. Ostrich on an illustration that I made, along with all of the rest of our beloved animals on it. (Please note that I use the terms bucking bronco, Ostrich, and Uncle Donny's

---

101. crass: lacking sensitivity, refinement, or intelligence.
102. mortal enemy: someone one hates very much and for a long time
103. emblem: a heraldic device or symbolic object as a distinctive badge of a nation, organization, or family.

interchangeably).

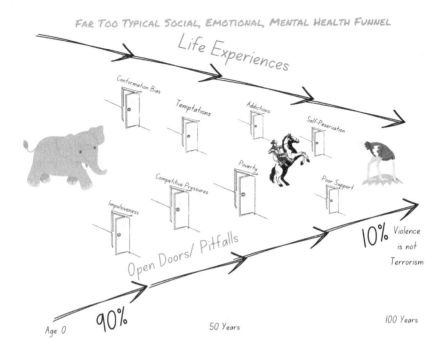

As illustrated, we all start out on our journeys with big ole beautiful and emotional elephant brains. As we travel down the road, we try to follow the "Chapter Four script" and practice "Chapter Four stuff," as best we can. Our little riders are fighting to stay in control, but for reasons we will continue to talk about, some percentage of us get sidetracked. It's hard to turn away from **excessiveness** as well as the many *temptations*[104] in life that test our **impulsive nature.** As we grow, that part of us that needs to satisfy a thirst for personal growth and ambition kicks into overdrive. The part of us that asks, "What about me?" rages within most of us, and puts us in **self-preservation** mode. American culture reinforces our outlook to strive to get ahead, make money, etc. We try to outdo each other and it's easy to become desensitized and uncaring. Our parents aren't perfect. Lots of us grow up absent sufficient guidance and without the opportunities to learn "Chapter Four" things. I haven't even

---

104. temptation: the desire to do something, especially something wrong or unwise.

talked about ***poverty.***[105] One can only begin to imagine the added number of pitfalls that those in poverty face. Then there is **alcohol and drugs.** Overuse can lead to the disease of **addiction** which often seals the deal. Addiction is *beguiling*[106]. Once gripped by the disease of addiction, it is very hard to realize what has become of us.(*Podcasts*, 2019) For most of our Bucking Broncos and Ostriches where there was once hope there is now despair. Where there was once gratitude there is now resentment.

Our broncos are a rare breed. However, I must admit lately it seems that they are growing in number and this has caused me at times to doubt my 10% theory. Worried about this, I have recently found myself asking family and friends about my theory. Many say that I'm being overly optimistic. I'm currently in the process of convincing my daughter... I was out to lunch with my pal Fitzy, (a Boston College alum, smart guy) I asked him, "Fitzy, would you agree that most people don't operate in the extremes? Am I crazy or is it true that people for the most part are helpful, they tell the truth and are equipped to help us solve the challenges in our society? Adding "I think the number is as high as 90% what do you think?"- Without a hesitation Fitz said to me "Glenn- My definition of being a good person, and your definition of being a good person may be different- but guess what- they aren't that different... Most people get it! " Fitzy gets it, and I'm almost positive that you get it because you are born with it. Thanks Fitzy, you saved my day.Following my pep talk with Fitzy, I left it on my chart that the people who lose their way are only about 10% of all of us. I can also cite statistical evidence for my 10% theory. See Footnote. (study that proves that as of 2022, 10% of registered voters support violence as a means of making change. (Pape, 2023)

However, as I said, it does seem as though we are seeing more of them in our daily lives lately. This needs to be accounted for.It used to be that a Bronco or an Ostrich stuck out like a sore thumb- something about them you can tell is just off. Overconfident, and opinionated when they have no cause to be, often negative, offering no solutions only problems. Sometimes their basic hygiene is off, but this is another story altogether.

---

105. poverty: the state of being extremely poor.
106. beguiling: charming or enchanting, often in a deceptive way.

Being a Bucking Bronco is a serious condition. Like an airplane that has lost its radar, our Broncos" antenna for regulating their emotions is damaged. They have become *disorientated*[107]- from what is right vs. wrong. The Bucking Bronco is that person in your life, that will disappoint you greatly, will dispute clear facts with you, will lie to you, or do worse. What is most scary about the Bronco, for the rest of us, is how he develops radical ideas and opinions which are not true, they are only made-up beliefs based on his own *distorted*[108] sense of reality. This has become our biggest threat of all.

Our broncos come in many shapes and sizes, some more obviously out of touch and pissed off than others. Many are just passively lost and moving through life aimlessly not helping... while the worst kind have become active in politics, and are willing to lie not caring about the consequences. They exist on a scale for sure, like many other things in life. But you can tell pretty quickly when you are dealing with someone who has lost his battle with their divided mind. For example, those of you who are old enough to drive might spot a badly beat-up Bucking Bronco on the highway, in their car, blasting music and riding by doing triple the speed limit while giving you "the finger" 🖕 for no reason. Sometimes, you can see the loss of their dignity in their eyes. They often look sad, and this makes me very sad. As they spew their disgust and *vitriol*[109] at me I think to myself, "but for the grace of God there go I" (Bradford & Townsend, 1842, p. xliii). The fact is that our 10%ers have traveled a tough road and couldn't overcome their circumstances.

I want to say one more thing about our Bronco's, using another metaphor I will call "the road of life." Picture a car traveling down a single-lane road losing traction, coming off center and slamming into the guardrail. Then flipping over, and crashing down the embankment (of life) and into a ditch. Please picture what can happen to a person who has lost his way. His car engine, smoking, his spirit broken, no friends, family, or loved ones in sight. He has been injured, now alone, confused, and disoriented. How vulnerable are they in this situation? If

---

107. disorientated: having lost one's sense of direction
108. distorted: giving a misleading or false account or impression; misrepresented.
109. vitriol: cruel and bitter criticism.

someone or something presented itself to them at that moment, wouldn't they tend to listen, grab hold, and latch on? I'm sure you know where I am going with this, this is what happens to our bucking broncos and many others who are just sad, lonely, and without direction or support in their lives. People in this hurt condition become prone to grab onto any person or group, even if that person or group stands for more of the same, another dark hole or a worse direction... Many lose trust in institutions built over thousands of years, they become their own arbiters of right and wrong. In the most injured form, Bronco's come to see themselves as judge and jury, questioning anything established by people before them. Some become *despots*[110] and *tyrants*[111], leaders of cults and movements. And a few become our criminals, and our mass shooters.

The fact is that most people who end up acting out against us were somehow along the line dealt a bad hand in life. They suffered some experiences that made them come off center, like returning from a war zone, or other traumatic event. None of this is their fault. It could happen to any one of us. When they take it out on you or me, it is only a reflection of themselves. That is why I choose not to blame them for being angry. I don't even blame them for some level of hate. There's a fine line between anger and hate. I don't blame anyone for who they are or what they've become, no matter what they've become.

Preventing people from losing the battle of the divided mind is the single most important thing that we can do together to improve our society. Your generation must ask the question- How do we keep people well? What makes you, my reader, a 90%er, is that you remain in touch with the goodness you were born with. We need to keep the light on within ourselves, in order to shine it upon others. The pages ahead will explain why prior generations have failed in this endeavor, and how future generations should be able to succeed. If I can help one of you recognize if and when you are heading down a path to becoming a Bronco, to regain your balance and maintain control over your emotions, this part of my book would be a huge success!

---

110. despot: a ruler or other person who holds absolute power, typically one who exercises it in a cruel or oppressive way
111. tyrant: a cruel and oppressive ruler

So please look back at the chart on page fifty-six, and remember how susceptible you are to falling into one of the traps. Also, I want to introduce a few other concepts here. There is nothing more dangerous for you (or all of us) than **excessive pride**. This may sound confusing so I have placed a definition of the word "pride" along with two other related phenomenons, which Dr. Haidt and other social psychologists call *cognitive biases*[112].

The three most important that I want to point out are **Excessive Pride, Confirmation bias, and Naive Realism.** Your being armed with these concepts, I hope, will help you be the best that you can be, and if we get this information to enough of you, we will reduce hate and help turn disagreement into compromise. We can teach empathy and compassion, and help people avoid becoming lost souls...

---

112. cognative bias: a systematic error in thinking that occurs when people are processing and interpreting information

Excessive Pride

Pride is the central vice. Pride is the problem with the sensory apparatus. Pride blinds us to the reality of our divided nature. Pride blinds us to our own weaknesses and misleads us into thinking we are better than we are. Pride makes us more certain and closed minded than we should be. Pride makes it hard for us to be vulnerable before those whose love we need. Pride makes coldheartedness and cruelty possible. Because of pride we try to prove we are better than those around us. Pride deprives us of our otherwise beautiful humility.

-David Brooks, The Road to Character

Conformation Bias

19th Century English physicist Michael Faraday described as human temptation "to seek for such evidence and appearances as are in the favor of our desires, and to disregard those which oppose them... We receive as friendly that which agrees with us, we resist with dislike that which opposes us; whereas the very reverse is required by every dictate of common sense" News organizations today leave out scientific facts that don't fit the desired narrative, a form of confirmation bias.

Naive Realism

the idea that the senses provide us with direct awareness of objects as they really are; also called direct realism

At this point, I've used almost every animal on the farm to describe our 10%. I think it's pretty clear that they exist. What to do about these people is less clear. Dr. Haidt, and modern brain doctors say that they have temporarily become imbalanced and that there is treatment. I agree, we do not want to give up on our Bronco's but I also think as our untreated Bronco's die off, we will eventually not have any more Bronco's. They will become extinct. A bit more on this plan later.

At this point, it's enough for me to ask you to recognize what they look like, and avoid becoming one! The great majority of us are doing the work, to remain hopeful and to keep the light on. We are following the Chapter 4 script, regardless of how boring or challenging it may be. Most of us show a willingness, day in and day out, to work with people with whom we disagree. But our broncos have disengaged from the work required of citizenship. They are unwilling to hear other people out, or to consider, even for a moment the error in their ways. Today our Bronco's are profoundly subtracting from my life experience and yours. Their doom and gloom attitudes control our society. So we need a plan to stop their rise.

The first part of my plan is to understand their sudden influence on the 90%. Two hundred years ago our society found a way to limit the number and effect of society's bucking bronco's. If a Bronco showed up and started in with crazy talk he was politely asked to leave until he could regain his manners. Maybe it was because the population was smaller, but there is no question, during the 18th century radical thinking was quieted and rational thinking was rewarded. Today, something has gone very wrong.

Not only have we let Uncle D back into the party, we handed him a microphone, a set of loudspeakers and gave him the largest audience that he would ever dream of. Now our crazy Uncle D's everywhere sit in their living rooms doing what they do best- *bloviating*[113]; getting off their chest everything that is wrong in their world and making themselves feel better. Our Uncle D's never let something as small as the truth, get in the way of a good story. In order for Uncle Donny to go "viral" he only needs to play on and stir up the emotions of his fellow extremists. Lies are rewarded with likes, shares, tweets, and reposts. Today lies are digested by millions, in seconds. When it comes to politics this manufactures fear and panic on both sides and creates class wars. Many of our Bronco's have nothing to lose by attacking people with reputation ruining lies, or threats of violence. The internet is such a dangerous place to communicate. If anyone tries to interrupt Uncle Donny when he gets going, they can be immediately embarrassed in front of millions, so most people don't get involved. What is left on our Televisions and on all forms of digital information are radical ideas, offered in soundbites, without factual support. A virtual cesspool of distortions of reality, and lies, mostly fueled by bitterness and

---

113. bloviate: talk at length, especially in an inflated or empty way

resentment. All repeated by the media, in a 24-hour, 7 days a week non-stop news loop. The noise that our 10% is making is deafening. We are being pummeled, drowned, and silenced by it.

When I sought independent verification of my assumptions about how destructive the internet has been it didn't surprise me that I found an article by my favorite psychologist. Wouldn't you know Dr. Haidt wrote an article that provided a detailed answer to the question -"Why the past 10 years of American Life Have Been Uniquely Stupid" (Haidt, 2022) Boy do I love this guy- he must have an Uncle Donny... In the article, Dr. Haidt confirms scientifically that social media has brought out the worst in us.

He writes, "As a social psychologist who studies emotion, morality and politics, I saw... The newly tweaked platforms were almost perfectly designed to bring out our... least reflective selves...with a naive conception of human psychology, little understanding of the intricacy of institutions, and no concern for the external costs imposed on society- Facebook, Twitter, YouTube, and a few other large platforms unwittingly dissolved the mortar of trust, belief in institutions, and shared stories that had held a large and diverse democracy together."(Haidt, 2022, p. 10) "YouTube has purposefully ignored warnings of its toxicity for years- even from its own employees- in pursuit of one value engagement... extremists have an easy time infiltrating social media and preying on people... Since these social services make money from attracting users and then selling those eyeballs to advertisers, they... design their algorithm not for safety but for... user stickiness. "The algorithms keep you glued to your screen by feeding you more of the content that they think you want...and they feed you content that is increasingly more extreme... sensationalist, since that is what drives clicks and keeps users". If you start out reading certain content that is tame ... it will eventually get you to content that is the most extreme, explicit, and violent, including those sites that incite violence and talk about doing violence...In this way, they serve as engines of polarization and pathways to radicalization."(Greenblatt, 2022, p. 109) "The key to designing a sustainable republic, therefore, was to build in mechanisms to slow things down, cool passions, and require compromise..." The internet does the opposite- it inflames our "most unruly passion" (Haidt, 2022, p. 11)

The reality is that it's almost never possible for a short blurb, to accurately depict someone's position on an issue, particularly when it's captured and spun by the media, and *sensationalized*[114], to look like something more or different than it actually is. Political issues are highly *nuanced*[115], requiring a delicate balancing act between many opposing viewpoints. We must know the details of the issues in order to form a rational opinion. But if we have learned anything from Dr. Haidt, it is that our first thoughts come from the elephant. Processing our initial reactions in order to get a more clear picture of reality is not something that we do well. Our first reaction always occurs in our "Brain Stem". As we process information more critically, we move it from the back of our brains to the frontal area, called the "Prefrontal cortex." This is where we begin to apply reason to emotion.

Think of it like our being an automobile with five gears. Our immediate reaction is us in first or second gear. When we move information from the brainstem to the frontal lobe it's like we are actively shifting from 2nd gear to 3rd, 4th, and 5th. In higher gears, we gather more facts, cool our passions and confront our biases. The more we can stay aware of this process in our brains, we develop the prefrontal area of our brains making us better at self-reflection, patience, teamwork, forgiveness, and problem-solving. In the case of the Bronco, they tend to stay in the "stem," and get stuck in what I will liken to our second gear. Our Broncos rarely if ever shift into higher gears. They do not take time to compare alternative viewpoints, research more facts, or apply conscious thinking. The conclusion: The information flowing on the internet is moving from "stem" to "stem," without the application of much or any rational thought. Our Uncle Donny's do not "THINK" that politics is complicated, rather they "FEEL" that it's simple. This is why they only see things in *binary*[116] terms. White people are the problem- Black people are the problem. Republicans are the problem, or Democrats are the problem. Today, you are either a winner or a loser, with America

---

114. sensationalize: present information about (something) in a way that provokes public interest and excitement, at the expense of accuracy.
115. nuance: a subtle difference in or shade of meaning, expression, or sound
116. binary: relating to, composed of, or involving two things

or against America, pro-police or anti-police, pro-immigrant or anti-immigrant. If you are fat or ugly- get over it- take the binky out of your mouth you little crybaby.

By allowing lies to flow freely, media, extremists, and political hyper-partisans, for the first time ever, have called into question all sources of truth. We had once been insulated from misinformation by trustworthy sources of information such as the New York Times newspaper, established in 1851. We have been stripped of the protection that credible sources of news once provided to us. **Our bucking broncos have successfully normalized the spreading of misinformation. By spreading lies about our sources of news, such as the New York Times and other longstanding news organizations themselves, they manage to *delegitimize*[117] fact-based media sources.** This also tends to delegitimize messages from our churches and synagogues as well. The normalization of lying is similar to normalizing crime. Once we allow these things into our society they become our everyday expectations. In this environment, it is hard to have confidence in right or wrong about anything. It's also a place where people on both sides have tuned each other out. Our national politics has become a "take the gloves off," "everything goes," "down and dirty" bar fight where everyone is losing.

We have entered a *vortex*[118] where people know that things are abnormal, but we somehow, inexplicably accept it, as our new normal. This is the place of indescribable noise and confusion that my students were trying to express to me. You may not have heard it explained in my terms, with the rise of the 10%, or as a big spinning wheel made up of cultural myths and *fallacies*[119], which is a new concept... but you feel it. You have come to know it is a place of historical significance. However, like the technology that is fueling it, it is very unfamiliar to us. So we have been stuck here for a while.

---

117. delegitimize: withdraw legitimate status or authority from (someone or something
118. vortex: a mass of whirling fluid or air, especially a whirlpool or whirlwind
119. fallacy: a mistaken belief, especially one based on unsound argument.

Many of us are sickened by what we are seeing yet we sit back and do nothing when we know in our heart what we are witnessing is so wrong. Following the Holocaust, after the war was over and 60 Million Jews were murdered along with untold numbers of children, Eleanor Roosevelt said, "We let our consciences realize too late the need of standing up against something we knew was wrong …we did nothing to prevent it." ("Eleanor Roosevelt Papers," in press) Philosopher Edmund Burke once said, "The only way evil succeeds is if good men do nothing." I realize how hard it is, particularly at your age, to stand up for things that we know are right. Taking an active role in making our government work is far more easily left for others. However, in this unengaged state, it is easy to get swept away by that aforementioned spinning wheel and unintentionally add momentum to it, *perpetuating*[120] wrong behaviors and unwittingly doing harm. The story of the rise of the 10%, is not as important as the story behind the fall of the 90%.

Our new normal itself can be the greatest opportunity for learning and regaining *universal*[121] sources of truth that there ever was. It can teach us that we are not being overtaken by corporate America, Russia or China, Facebook, or the big bad wolf. We are doing these things to ourselves, so this is not someone else's problem to fix. So now is the time to tell the rest of the story. How do 90% of the people get overtaken by the 10%?

There wasn't one moment or event that took us to this scary place, with real Uncle Donny's (and a few well-known Aunt Delores') roaming the halls of Congress, bickering nonsense back and forth all over our TVs and making most of us sick. It would take a coming together of a few factors to get us to a place worth writing a book about. I hope that by reflecting upon the circumstances in some detail, first by looking at the basic ingredients, and then a "play by play", the new normal itself will reveal the types of everlasting truths that I promised you at the outset of the book.

---

120. perpetuate: make (something, typically an undesirable situation or an unfounded belief) continue indefinitely
121. universal: of, affecting, or done by all people or things in the world or in a particular group; applicable to all cases

Chapter 7: Our Unraveling- Basic Ingredients and Natural Law

I want to start this chapter by confirming some assumptions that I've made about you, my reader. First, I assume that you know what someone I have called "our crazy Uncle Donny" looks and acts like. Second, I assume that you have followed along identifying with the people who I have called Bronco's and Ostriches. These assumptions both rest upon a larger theory on which all my hopes and dreams for your future success rely on. It's a belief system called the Natural Law. Much has been written about the natural law and much of the rest of this book will be spent trying to convince you of its existence and of the dangers of violating it. If it were taught in school it would have three prerequisite courses. Natural Law 101 is the foundation and it is as powerful as it is simple. It says that human beings are divinely created with the ability to *reason*[122], to apply logic and evidence to the world in front of us and reach common-sense conclusions, unlike any other animal in the world. Cicero was one of the first to define reality in terms of natural laws, when he said, "The Creator's order of things is called the Natural Law. A fundamental presupposition of the natural law is that man's reasoning power is a special dispensation of the Creator and is closely akin to the rational or reasoning power of the Creator himself..."(Skousen, 1981, p. 39)"The animal which we call man, endowed with foresight and quick intelligence, complex, keen, possessing memory, full of reason and prudence, has been given a certain distinguished status by the Supreme God who created him; for he is the only one among so many different kinds of varieties of living beings who has a share in reason and thought, while all the rest are depraved of it."(Skousen, 1981, p. 41)This statue, by Auguste Rodin, (1880) is a visual expression that "man is a uniquely reflective and self-aware animal, and that this is something fundamental to the human condition."(Magee, 2016, p. 7).

---

122. reason: the power of the mind to think, understand, and form judgments by a process of logic.

If Natural Law 101 holds true, then I don't have to explain to you what our society would look like if a **real Uncle Donny** became President of the United States of America. You were born with the common sense to know that our new normal is a place that is only made possible by such a circumstance.

Yet, in January of 2016, that is exactly what happened. A REAL Uncle Donny and someone who I am quite sure would not mind in the least being called a bucking bronco, took the main stage as the 45th President. What could go wrong... right? I don't mean any disrespect to "The Donald" (I don't think he minds being called that either...) but I have a strong hunch that even if you are a Donald Trump supporter you know what I mean. I take no position on who or what you should believe politically, and as I hope you will come to realize, I don't blame Mr Trump for anything. Correct that, let me clarify and say that if I were to blame him for anything, it's the same thing that I blame myself for. More on this later.

Natural Law 102 is the belief in what the ancient philosophers called _Cosmopolitanism[123]_. It is the observance that all human beings live interconnected lives and it matters greatly how we treat one another. The idea of our being interconnected in some way with people we do not know may be best summarized by the words from the Bible. The book of Paul indicates that there is a Supreme Creator of all things and that all humans share his spirit. (Gomes, 2009, p. 235) "To each is given the manifestation of the Spirit for the common good" (Corinthians12:7). "For by one Spirit we were all baptized into one body- Jews and Greeks, slaves or free- and all were made to drink of one Spirit." Paul speaks of "the higher gifts... three theological virtues of faith, hope, and love." Paul says that if we live under the protective umbrella of one spirit, and live by the gifts he has given us, that we will prosper together. In the Bible it is written, "earnestly desire the higher gifts and I will show you a more excellent way." (Corinthians12:12) And this you may have heard also from the catholic faith ; "Love thy neighbor as you do yourself, and do unto others as you would have done unto you." (Galatians 5:14). The world's religions interpret _providential_ laws such that there is a grand scheme of things which we are not to take lightly. Philosophers translated the message to politics; "To Cicero, ... the only reliable basis for sound government and just human relations is Natural Law... (Skousen, 1981, p. 37) "The building of a society on principles of Natural Law was nothing more or less than recognizing and identifying the rules of "right conduct" with the laws of the Supreme Creator of the universe.``(Skousen, p. 39) Cicero said, "The glue which holds a body of human beings together in the commonwealth of a just society is love... love of one's fellow man which provides the desire to promote true justice among mankind" and "man's

---

123. cosmopolitanism: the ideology that all human beings belong to a single community, based on a shared morality

ability to organize government originates in our sharing a belief in the ultimate goodness of mankind…this is the foundation of justice" (Skousen, p. 39). Without this fundamental belief, we have no basis to form any functioning government or for there to be any just relations between human beings.

The natural law therefore begins with two types of moral ties, a commitment we make to ourselves, and a commitment we make to others. It is also a two-step process. Step one is all about maintaining awareness of our higher gifts, and acting upon them. **If we don't use our gifts we lose our gifts. Some refer to this as "self-mastery" and there are a few concepts in this book more important than this one because a better society is built by better people, and a society doesn't unravel until its individual participants do first.**

In his book, "How to Think Like a Roman Emperor." Dr. Donald Robertson, a Ph.D. in cognitive psychotherapy (brain function) chronicles the life of Marcus Aurelius emperor of Rome, a student and practitioner of what is called Stoic Philosophy. Stoic philosophy and natural law hold many themes in common. They are both outlooks on life which advocate for certain redeeming truths. About step one, maintaining our God-given gifts, Dr. Robertson writes, "The Stoics can teach you how to find a sense of purpose in life, how to face adversity, how to conquer anger within yourself, moderate your desires, experience healthy sources of joy, endure pain and illness patiently and with dignity, exhibit courage in the face of your anxieties, cope with loss, and perhaps even confront your own mortality while remaining as unperturbed as Socrates." "There is a treasure trove of spiritual practices, tucked away in the literature of Greek and Roman philosophy, which were clearly designed to help people overcome emotional suffering and develop strength of character… When we take it on as a philosophy of life, with daily practice, we have the opportunity to learn greater emotional resilience, strength of character, and moral integrity."(Robertson, 2019, p. 14) Similar to the way we do push-ups or sit-ups to make our body strong, Stoic philosophy teaches us how to work on our mind in order to protect and nourish the moral fabric which is embedded in each of our souls.

Step two of Natural law, which I will continue to refer to as belief in Cosmopolitanism, asks us to recognize that the virtue we develop in ourselves is intended to be shared with others. Cosmopolitanism requires that we set as one of our purposes in life to get along with other people because we contribute to other's pain, or fortune, far more than we may realize. Dr. Robertson ties together part one of nature's laws with part two when he writes, "The Stoics believed that as we mature in wisdom we increasingly identify with our own capacity for reason, but we also begin to identify with others insofar as they're capable of reason. In other words, the wise man extends moral consideration to all rational creatures and views them, in a sense, as his brothers and sisters...The stoics described their ideal as cosmopolitanism, or "being citizens of the same universe," a phrase attributed both to Socrates and Diogenes... Stoic ethics involve cultivating this natural affection toward other people in accord with virtues like justice, fairness, and kindness. Although this social dimension of Stoicism is often overlooked today, it's one of the main themes of The Meditations (Marcus Aurelius' journal). Marcus touches on topics such as the virtues of justice, and kindness , natural affection, the brotherhood of man, and ethical cosmopolitanism on virtually every page." (p41 How To Think Like a Roman Emperor). It's all about gaining what has been called a collective consciousness, or a shared way of thinking about the world. Walk into any church, synagogue, mosque, or other place of religion and you will hear of these *tenets*[124] of natural law. For example, in Africa, they teach the philosophy of *Ubuntu*[125] which reminds believers that "I am because we are."

Even if you aren't into religion or philosophy, it's not hard to believe that there is a natural course to things. For example; there is a reason why when someone (a health nut like my sister n law) gives you chocolate pudding made from Avocados, that it doesn't taste like chocolate pudding- because as you know, chocolate pudding made from Avocados isn't chocolate pudding at all- it's avocado pudding!

Let me give you another example from when I coached Mikey in Little League when he was 10 years old. He had this weird, but

---

124. tenet: a principle or belief, especially one of the main principles of a religion or philosophy
125. Ubuntu: a quality that includes the essential human virtues; compassion and humanity

lovable, little friend named Oliver who always sat on the bench and he seemed thrilled about it, probably because he would strike out every time he got to bat and couldn't catch the ball… but everyone liked Oliver including me. When I think about today's great political divide and all of the distrust and misunderstanding in our country today I have this recurring daydream or nightmare if they can happen during the day? (Cue the music and clouds please, this time add friendly chirping birds) …I get to the park one day and Oliver approaches me and says "Mr. Cort, please take a seat on the bench. I am coaching today." (end music and chirping birds here) All of us know what would happen if Oliver was our coach. Great ice cream parties, yes. Playing baseball not so much.

So too at a young age, we understand that our leaders in business or government need to have certain qualities which qualify them for the role. We know that leaders are the protectors of truth. We know that honesty, integrity, and selflessness, are the values which hold up any organization- a family, a community, and a government. As we mature we come to understand that the larger and more complex the system the more important this concept becomes. **Lies make it impossible for people to communicate. A leader who allows misinformation to spread and conspiracy theories to go unchecked ensures the destruction of that organization. It's not a matter of whether its participants will come to distrust each other, and tear the organization down, it's only a matter of when. When a lie is repeated enough, it begins to look like the truth. Therefore, if you want to tear down any system that relies on people, just start lying.**

But we forget things don't we? Even the most fundamental of things like this. That is unless we are really paying attention. Allowing dangerous lies to go unchecked was the biggest mistake Mr. Trump made during his presidency. The other was his arrogance, but this chapter will not be all about Mr. Trump. In fact, to blame Mr. Trump would defeat the whole purpose of the book, which is to reveal truth.

The truth is that Mr. Trump behaved like an ordinary person while he was President and it is this "ordinariness" that exists in our culture, which we allow for without fully understanding the consequences, that is doing most if not all of our harm. Donald

Trump is not a bad person, regardless of what you may have heard or what you are being told. What we must learn is that Mr. Trump is a _perfect example of a person who is stuck in second gear, (in violation of NL 101) and blind to the impact of his own shortsightedness (in violation of NL 102)._ There is nothing terribly wrong with being in second gear, at times in your life. In fact, you could probably spend your whole life in second gear and not do too much harm, that is unless you want to be a leader of anything. As I said earlier, the threshold for being a good person is FAR lower than being a good citizen, and that is FAR lower than what it takes to be a politician.

I have come to believe that Politics is our Kryptonite. I'm assuming you all know the story of Superman and how Kryptonite works? It's that one thing that brought Superman to his knees. Politics has a unique way of shrinking us humans to our most ordinary and lowest life forms because it requires that we take things from each other. It's a game of give and take, and because everyone has a different opinion of how much to give and how much to take, it's the hardest thing we are forced to do together. It's not like this giving and taking is happening between a small family or group of friends. It's easy to get along in small groups. Amongst your friends or a small group of people, you can say whatever you want, if a "fistfight" breaks out nobody is going to get seriously hurt. Feelings are easily mended in small groups. In small numbers, for example in private clubs or small towns, there is not a lot of room, _literally_[126] and or _figuratively_[127], for misunderstanding. However, as groups of people expand into massive societies the room for disagreements between people balloons to equal the size and complexion of the group; and when we add diversity of backgrounds and colors, the room for disagreement multiplies _exponentially_[128]. Therefore, it should be easy for everyone to understand that it takes a very special person with _extraordinary_ intelligence and prolonged education to navigate this complexity. Just as there are basic ingredients to making a great pork chop, there are basic ingredients to effective leadership. When someone doesn't know the ingredients, or the right temperature under which those ingredients come together to

---

126. literal: taking words in their usual or most basic sense without metaphor or allegory
127. figurative: departing from a literal use of words; metaphorical
128. exponentially: (of an increase) becoming more and more rapid

make a great result, the results suck. The problem is that making government work is substantially harder than baking a perfect pork chop! What we are seeing today in America, is when it comes to governing systems as complex as ours, the wrong cook in the kitchen will cause a major explosion.

Most of us don't have what it takes to be a politician, including myself. I am currently trying to earn the title but for many years I was stuck in second gear. Regretfully, that didn't stop me from sitting around with my friends and calling our politicians morons. Most of us make fun of our elected leaders via texts, and email, sending our hateful and demeaning "memes." We demonize them for ruining our lives and blame them for our problems in society- when it's really our own fault. It took me fifty-four years to come to realize that it's people like me who are the source of our problems. After high school and college, I went directly into the business world to chase the almighty dollar. I never stepped foot back into a library after leaving school, to read about religion, history, philosophy, or the events which told the story of how and why our great country was formed. When I stepped into the voting booth and nobody was watching, I did what millions of other ordinary citizens do, I placed my own good ahead of the common good. For years, I didn't engage in my community, instead, I sat back and watched as we elected more and more typically flawed and uninspiring leaders, every year. They have led our country right down into the shitter. I made it okay. for our leaders to be as weak and ineffective as I have been as a citizen.

It is easy for a wide gap to open between who we become and who we were meant to become. It's easy to forgive yourself as you go through life not paying much attention, if any, to the government or your actual role in society. It wasn't until I finally went to the library and read the words and letters about our truly amazing founding fathers, that I realized the harm I have caused by being so ordinary, unaware, and careless of the truths that really matter. Recently, however, in seeing what is happening to our country, witnessing the onslaught of hate and disgust people have grown for each other, I've grown heartsick, and become embarrassed for all of us. It's hard for me to see my kids watch the television while politicians demean each other, and trample on the graves of our forefathers who knew so much more than people realize, or give credit to today. I now realize what I have done in behaving like such a commoner. So who am I to blame Mr. Trump for underestimating how his *uncompromising*[129] and theatrical style and exaggerations of truth would fuel existing fires and bring out the worst in our complex society? Barely any of us are paying close enough attention.

I feel like I turned my life around by going to the library and reading like I did. There I could feel myself mentally shifting into higher gears as I read about our history, about our founding fathers and about their faith in us. Today, I realize how different it is, being stuck in second gear, versus someone who finds a way to shift into third and fourth. I realize that the higher gears can accurately be called insight and foresight. This is when I had my awakening. **Our losing sight of how hard self-government is and our not taking full account and measurement of our ordinariness is doing most, if not all of our harm.**

Natural Law 103 may not be as widely written about, yet for me, it provides the most compelling proof of the existence of a *predestined*[130] path for human conduct. NL 103 is all about the beauty and *magnificence*[131] of nature itself. Most human beings agree that the beauty we partake of in nature is a force unto itself and something to be *reconciled*[132] with. When immersed in mother nature some of us walk away feeling like we matter more, some walk away feeling like we matter less; but all walk away with a similar sense of exhilaration, wonder, and awe. We become *contemplative*[133] in nature, asking ourselves the questions about life that are most elusive- What is the meaning of it all? Why am I here? What is my purpose? So what is this magical force that so many of us are drawn to? Is Mother Nature trying to tell us something? Of course, she is. I believe there are two main lessons that are revealed by the splendor of Mother Nature.

---

129. uncompromising: showing an unwillingness to make concessions to others, especially by changing one's ways or opinions
130. predestined: (of an outcome or course of events) determined in advance by divine will or fate
131. magnificence: impressively beautiful, elaborate, or extravagant; striking
132. reconcile: restore friendly relations between
133. contemplative: expressing or involving prolonged thought.

First, <u>we were not meant to be ordinary</u>. The word 'ordinary' means, *"with no special or distinctive features."* This is not us. The earth and human beings were all given existence by the same creator, it's not logical that we should have any less potential to be extraordinary than nature is. It follows that we have the same potential in us, as she has in her.

Secondly, can anyone dispute that nature represents all those things that we will never know? No one knows how we got here or who made us. I hope you will agree that this statement falls under the category of undeniable fact. The earth existed thousands of years before us and will live for thousands of years to follow. Our universe is as large as a single grain of sand on an endless beach. All one needs to do is look to the sky on a clear night to see the sheer size and overwhelming mystery of it all. It's hard not to be humbled by nature. In fact, only such an *immeasurable*[134] force as the great unknown can humble us the way that it does, and that is where the second lesson lies; **The great unknown provides us with a clear directional signal to the most essential of human qualities, which is humility. The humility we feel in nature taps directly into our intelligence, almost by some miracle, it sets us on a righteous path which enables us to get along splendidly with all other creatures.**

To summarize NL 103: Ordinary is not our intended condition. In our most natural form, human beings are meant to be as extraordinary as Mother Nature herself. We were meant to be humble and not arrogant.

At this moment I wish to give you what feels to me like a *prophetic*[135] gift. Before giving it to you, I would like first to thank all the authors of the books I read that have allowed me to arrive at this moment. Here goes: Only a philosopher can be a politician. It will also require each of us to learn the basics of natural law, (and the principles of stoic philosophy) in order for us to meet the goals I've set forth in this book. This may sound like a big ask, but it isn't. All our founding fathers were philosophers who believed in natural law. Each of them believed that our republic sits upon a delicate foundation of individual

---

134. immeasurable: too large, extensive, or extreme to measure
135. prophetic: accurately describing or predicting what will happen in the future

competencies which are taught and learned, won or lost, and not easily kept or maintained. They knew that self-government would fail if people were stuck in second gear.

The word 'Philosopher' itself, comes from the Greek word Philos, and means lover of wisdom. Philosophers created the word education itself and built our first schools. Philosophers painstakingly seek truth, and speak it, even when it doesn't serve their own interests. Philosophers attach themselves to the principles of self-awareness (or self-mastery- NL 101) and the law of cosmopolitanism (NL 102). They apply themselves to these tenets of natural law by force of their minds. None say that it is easy. They never stop believing in the miracle which is self-improvement. Philosophers live in a constant state of awareness of their own shortcomings. They are continuously working through the many cognitive distortions that enter their minds.

Being a politician requires a person to work tirelessly each day, in duty to his fellow man (and never to himself or his own group) to move heaps of information from his elephant brain to his more developed brain, to apply rational thought and evidence before reaching conclusions. Philosopher as Politician is an idea whose time came but went, and we need to get it back, soon. Ever since the word politician became known in America for being something negative, we have settled for ordinary in our leaders. We have been in a downward spiral ever since.

We don't see the results of our acting inconsistently with natural law, or being stuck in second gear, immediately- it creeps up on us. First, we become tired of each other, then we offend each other, then we stop caring for each other, and then we hate each other. Hate is the *ultimate*[136] expression of the failure of God's plan. It represents the complete loss of our natural-born abilities to reason and gain foresight and insight. **Hate represents us in our most unnatural form.** Hate is telling anyone who ever wrote a book about natural law to go screw themselves. Hate is failure of purpose, and failure of meaning which leads to a loss of identity. On a micro level our haters feel this loss of identity and sense of failure and act on it.

Below on the page, I have drawn a scale. On the far left-hand

---

136. ultimate: the best achievable or imaginable of its kind

side, you will see the word Hater. On the far right-hand side, you will see the word Philosopher. In the middle, you will see an Ordinary person. It's important to remember that **there are no lesser people, there are only lesser states of cognitive functioning and awareness.**

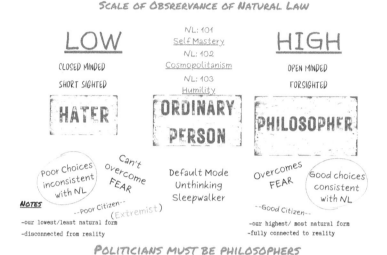

When we get stuck in second gear -in default mode- (See Middle of the Scale) we get stuck feeling our way through life rather than thinking our way through it. You remember my bird story? In this mode, we begin to manipulate facts for their own purposes. I am currently in the process of moving to the Right on the scale… I hope you will join me.

It is only by moving to the right on the scale in the belief in natural law 101, that people gain intellectual humility. "At the personal level, intellectual humility counterbalances narcissism, self-centeredness, pridefulness, and the need to dominate others. Conversely, intellectual humility seems to correlate positively with empathy, responsiveness to reasons, the ability to acknowledge what one owes (including intellectually) to others, and the moral capacity for equal regard of others. Arguably its ultimate fruit is a more accurate understanding of oneself and one's capacities."(Blankenhorn, 2019)

There are many reasons why people become unattached to the natural law and get stuck. It's critical that we understand why.

Cicero may have summed up things best, when over 2000 years ago, when he said, "As one and the same Nature holds together and supports the universe, all of whose parts are in harmony with one another, so men are united in Nature; but by reason of their own depravity they quarrel, not realizing that they are of one blood and subject to one and the same protecting power. If this fact were understood, surely man would live the life of the gods!"(Skousen, 1981, p. 46)

So what are these depravities that Cicero spoke of so long ago? It's as if he had an iPhone and simply called Dr. Haidt to consult with him, "Yo Dr. H tell me everything you and modern brain doctors have learned about the flaws in the human brain? I think there's some serious shit going on with us that is getting in the way of our getting along, but I am not quite sure. It's the year 43BC here, and I'm sitting on a rock bench, and working by a candle. I was hoping you could help me out". These guys were separated by 2000 years but saying the exact same thing!

You recall, Dr. Haidt said that our initial reactions, first impressions, thoughts, and ideas are mostly based on primal or instinctive fear. Have you ever given a speech in front of your class or to a large audience, and felt fear? If you are like me, not only do you become fearful, you start imagining all the worst possible outcomes. Science tells us that our immediate reactions are almost always great overreactions. That is why, in the case of public speaking, we start thinking that the people in the audience don't care for us, or that they want us to fail. We actually begin to imagine them as our enemies. When that isn't true at all. **The bottom line is that we tend to greatly exaggerate our fears, and imagine things that are not true.** I recently heard a behavioral therapist say that the acronym for "FEAR" is only False Evidence Appearing Real. It takes an unbelievable amount of effort, preparation to get yourself in the right mindset to give a speech. We will always succumb to our first fears unless we kick into a much higher state of awareness and cognitive function. When stuck in our ordinary state of consciousness we don't look fear in the face and overcome it, rather it overtakes us.

Earlier in the book I made a big deal about a condition called Narcissism. Narcissism, like anxiety and depression, is recognized by the medical community as being a state of impaired mental health. Because they are recognized by the medical community we invest millions in taxpayer dollars to help people recover from them. (US Department of Health and Human Services [HHS], 2022) People in these states are suffering from imagined fears which they cannot control. The demons they battle are all unwanted, and made up in their minds. "anxiety disorders" affect 40 Million adults every year, making it the most common mental illness in the US. Nearly 30% of adults experience symptoms of an anxiety *disorder*[137] at some point in their lives. (Lifeskills South Florida, 2023) However, when it comes to intolerance, arrogance, and ignorance, these conditions become safeguarded as some type of American right when they are clearly forms of sub-optimal cognitive functioning.

Angry parents that yell over people at school meetings, they don't seem happy. They look anxious and even depressed to me. My common sense tells me that they are suffering from a temporary sub-optimal state of cognitive impairment. I feel badly for them. People who say in public that they "hate our President, and wish him dead," (whether he is Donald Trump or Joe Biden) but who cannot cite any policy details in support of their *ardent*[138] position, they seem to me to be acting out of some type of fear. We are suffering from different forms of mental health problems. Most of our fears are *figments*[139] of an overactive imagination. These are the basic ingredients to our unraveling.

In his book, The Everyday Patriot, Author Tom Morris writes, **"Hurt People, Hurt People."** He describes people stuck in a lower gear of cognitive awareness saying, "They've accepted false goods, poisonous inner feelings, and orientations that have brought them a poor counterfeit of happiness based on a mistaken sense of self-righteousness and superiority to others. They can't manage to release this in order to enter a great community of true happiness and fellowship that's openly

---

137. disorder: a state of confusion

138. ardent: enthusiastic or passionate

139. figments: a thing that someone believes to be real but that exists only in their imagination

available to them…" And then he says inquisitively, "We need to release <u>whatever is holding us back</u>, let go of all the negativities that have sadly come to define our time… "(Morris, 2023, p. 4) The science says, what is holding us back most is fear- the fear that ordinary people have for other ordinary people.I have my own theories, not so much based on science but my own common sense and life experiences as to why we detach from such basic, obvious, and natural laws.

First, as we know, when we are born we have a very accurate sense of right from wrong. Therefore, when things do not go according to the plan, for example, if our parents mistreat us, or society does not support us the way it should we know that there is something very wrong with this and that is why we pull away and detach. I think it's totally normal that we should develop a sense of resentment for authority and an uncaring attitude about government as we grow older. Think about it, for our whole lives we are being told what to do. By our parents, siblings, grandparents, teachers, coaches, clergy, bosses, spouses, and on and on, by the time we reach our late 20s or early 30s, we've had a few jobs, we become tired of being told what to do Not only that, when we reach a certain age we figure that we know pretty much everything that we are going to know. We reach a stage when we don't want to be told what is right or wrong about anything, particularly by strangers in a system of government that we learned little about in school. In this state of, "I am who I am and you aren't gonna change me," we casually, and often unknowingly contribute to the negative attitudes about government that everyone else in society seems to have. And then there is the final stage that takes us over the edge.

Our resentments turn into a sense of entitlement. These feelings of entitlement are what begin to shape our definition of what American freedom means, and this is when, and how and why we really start to kick the shit out of each other. Let me explain. I believe that most of the people who are heckling people off of podiums and cursing each other out at public school meetings know deep down that what they are doing is wrong. We all have a super strong sense of right and wrong and what gives us the uncanny ability to know there is a time and a place for everything. In those moments, they figure that society deserves it and that they deserve a few moments to be heard for having to put up with other human beings for so long. They also figure that their one or two moments of *indiscretion*[140] will not amount to a hill of beans. However, this is where things take a huge turn for the worst… and which people don't realize. Each citizen's singular momentary lapse in discretion makes a huge difference because there are so many of us who are taking the same pleasurable time outs from being good. Collectively these all too common emotional outbursts, direct from the brain stem, without conscious thought, are all adding up in our society, to define who we are. Our kids learn from these moments and slowly begin to think that it is how they are supposed to act. This is the start of kids taking on our worst form, and they don't see what is happening to them. Politicians, who have not yet learned how to think like a Roman Emperor, who are stuck in second gear, interrupt other politicians out of their sense of entitlement, and uncontrolled emotional anger, and this is what becomes normalized in our society.

Even our most recent president of the US, Joe Biden, was interrupted and called a liar in the middle of giving his nationally televised annual State of the Union address to Congress. It's not that he is or isn't a liar, that is not the point, it's that there is a time and place for everything, and when we fail to self-master (gain control over our worst instincts) and forget about cosmopolitanism (how we impact each other) we all go to dark place together!

We tend to grow up and not think about any of this stuff right ? Or if anything we grow to think that the way we act should not be anyone else's business. This is the world of Me, instead of the world of We that we are living in today. This is the America we live in today- Where our lowest moments define who we are. **These are the modes, and the mindsets that we slip into.** That the government sucks and that American freedom means that we can do or say whatever the hell we want, are two of the largest cultural lies that have kept us divided for years.

People do not make a conscious choice to become stuck in second gear, in the same way, they do not choose to become overwhelmed by anxiety or depression. Our loss of ability to be great citizens is often an invisible process, it is one that the

---

140. indiscretion: behavior or speech that is indiscreet or displays a lack of good judgment

person who is failing to realize his gifts cannot see. Much of our anger is naturally occurring, it's hard to check ourselves. But it's a frighteningly fast slide we take if we are not given the support we need to see through the *speculation[141]*, *innuendo[142]*, *conjecture[143]*, and conspiracy theories that divide people…

In terms of what it looks like to be stuck in our most ordinary and fearful state- it looks bad. If we were a laundry machine we would have our "dial" set to "Automatic -common man approach & SPIN." I've drawn the dial below.

We wake up and eat breakfast, if politics comes up our natural "reflexes" kick in. We don't look for information that would counter our own position. Instead, we impulsively take the same position we had yesterday. We hate the other side for what we **THINK** that they believe, even though it's most likely we don't understand half of what they stand for. We choose news sources which reinforce the current picture we have in our head, we have dinner and go to bed. The next day we wake up and do it all over again. Unless we move further up the scale a person cannot and will not stop to realize the harm they are doing each day. Things that could unite a society, such as the natural law get washed away in something that very much resembles a laundry machine spin cycle. **This is the society we have now- We are fighting a war of extremes between mostly imagined enemies!**

---

141. speculation: the forming of a theory or conjecture without firm evidence
142. innuendo: an allusive or oblique remark or hint, typically a suggestive or disparaging one
143. conjecture: an opinion or conclusion formed on the basis of incomplete information

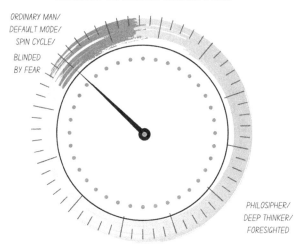

SPIN CYCLE OF FEAR

AUTOMATIC –COMMON MAN APPROACH + SPIN

ORDINARY MAN/
DEFAULT MODE/
SPIN CYCLE/

BLINDED
BY FEAR

PHILOSIPHER/
DEEP THINKER/
FORESIGHTED

INSTRUCTIONS:
WE HAVE CURRENTLY SET OUR DIAL TO COMMON MAN/ DEFAULT MODE.
THIS IS AN AUTOMATIC SPIN CYCLE CAUSING RADICAL IDEAS TO TEAR AT OUR MORAL FABRIC.

DETERGENT:
ORDINARY MINDSET, IRRATIONAL FEARS, BLINDNESS, HATE,

CAUTION:
SPIN CYCLE CAN CAUSE A WAR OF EXTREMES BETWEEN
IMAGINED ENEMIES. USE AS DIRECTED.

The last time I was in the library, darkness had just fallen, and the cavernous building was dimly lit... I felt this weird but eerily cool feeling wash over me- as if all of the books in the library started talking to me at once, I felt the weight of thousands of years of history wash over me as a single *resounding*[144] voice spoke to me, (cue the deep voice and church bells in the background of this dream- No chirping birds please) It said, "Glenn... there are common denominators in all our pages- Think about the common themes Glenn... Get to the young

---

144. resounding: unmistakable; emphatic.

people, as their minds are still open, the mass of all of the information in this library, in the hundreds and thousands of pages within these walls, and of the thousands of authors mostly dead or dying and those still young enough to deliver a book to these shelves. Take our combined truth and give it to the kids- they badly need to know of our message, and we cannot all be wrong!!!" (echo, echo, echo) WOW. It was an amazing moment. Such a feeling can feel like the weight of the world has dropped on your shoulders. It's scary to think that you actually have figured something out, but you know, at that moment, that other people may not believe you. Especially something as large as - <u>knowing that there actually is a single source of truth in this world.</u> But then there are times when I think I can pull it off, when I think to myself- how could all these voices be wrong?

From that night on, I started to think about how I could possibly relay, as fact, or prove- that the natural law is the only source of truth and authority.

Of course, proving that there is one set of guidelines to proper human conduct is not an easy task. However, because all the books in the library had asked me too, I have to give it my best try.

When I was in New York City I snapped this photo of Saint Patrick's Cathedral. It seemed to stand for the type of stability we need. There are thousands of these monuments across our country, which took hundreds of years to build, and millions of people flock to them daily. I want to ask you to wonder as I do, if the multitudes of people dedicated to building those places of worship did so for reasons that are not important for us to think about? Is it actually reasonable for us to think that they have all been wasting their time? Of course not. Can't we muster enough faith in each other to realize that as humans we seek to be good and that we are, actually all in this together? Can't we ever stop to think that our longstanding institutions are long-standing for a reason and that inside them there is a source of universal truth?

The bottom line is that there is truth, there is normal and there is right and wrong- It all runs according to natural law. That it is what all of the books in the library boil down to. It is the basis of all moral and political philosophy and it is also the basis for *patriotism*[145]. One cannot believe and follow the natural laws and not be a good patriot. I've checked it twice like Santa Clause would. Who knows maybe other life forms will visit us someday or maybe God himself or herself, or Santa, will pay us a visit and change the rules but until then we only have one choice. Follow the natural law. It has been thousands of years that philosophers, historians, and leaders of organized religion have been trying to tell us, and we have not listened. **We are failing to follow the rules and very bad things are happening to us. It is that simple.**

The older generation has lost its way. But that is okay. We will soon be in your past. At your age, you have not lost your ability to learn and grow. There is every reason to believe that your generation will grow up to retain your God-given gifts, by coming to understand what it takes to do so. When a future generation makes it a priority for every American born to retain their gifts and learn how to think like a Roman emperor, you will, as Cicero said, finally live the life of the Gods.

---

145. patriotism: the quality of being patriotic; devotion to and vigorous support for one's country

Chapter 8: The Play-by-Play

I have to tell you something. I realize how unpopular it is to claim that there is absolute truth, about anything. Even if it's something as simple as Oliver shouldn't coach, your crazy Uncle Donny shouldn't be President, or that chocolate pudding made with avocado sucks. I realize that my speaking in such absolute terms about natural laws may come across as one of those nasty ISMs. Like nationalism, populism, communism, totalitarianism, authoritarianism, fascism, or more recently "wokism"; but given how weird things have gotten in our society, I can't help myself.

I was already feeling a little uncomfortable with my speaking in such absolute terms, and then recently I stumbled upon the word "postmodernity" and it has only made my discomfort grow. Postmodernity, the article said "*as* a worldview, refuses to allow any single defining source for truth and reality. It is the wholesale rejection of universal reason and absolute truth... In the present, postmodern era, there is no single defining source for truth and reality beyond the individual. Claims of universal meaning are viewed as *imperialistic*[146] efforts to *marginalize*[147] and oppress the rights of others... it is the inadmissibility of all totalizing ways of viewing any dimension of life... There is no objective reality. There is only the individual's subjective view of truth and reality."(Cornell, 2006) I thought about this for a second and even put my pencil down for a minute. Then I thought more deeply about today's politics. No matter what anyone else tells you, **we are losing at the hands of only one ISM, and that is <u>extremISM.</u>** Oh shoot- There I go again... I know that there needs to be some serious justification for me to continue to do this.

I want you to know that I realize that even if I were to convince 100% of my readers of the reasons WHY we have reached a low point -Hint: by violating the natural laws and giving life to extremISM- that fixing things is a totally different story. I realize that there are important questions to be answered such as- what

---

146. imperialistic: a policy of extending a country's power and influence through diplomacy or military force
147. marginalize: treat (a person, group, or concept) as insignificant or peripheral

do we do with the people who will never agree with natural law? I have reserved some space to answer that question. At this point in the proceedings, however, I want to focus on how our violations of natural law are playing out in real life. I want to start with a little historical background. This includes taking a detailed look at the participants who are fighting in our war of extremes, and a summary of the actual events that took us to the place we find ourselves in. Then, true to form, I will end the chapter by making MORE absolute statements of truth!

Since the birth of our American form of government, called a Republic, we've always had two parties who stand in opposition on a main issue, that is the size and reach of government. The origins of our two-party system is worth discussing briefly, but before jumping there, I want to first pose a fundamental question. Why do we have a Federal Government at all? It's not that you don't know this, but I figure that things have gotten so out of control that a quick refresher will not offend you, and will hopefully help frame things. I want to start by setting out our ideal situation. The perfect situation is that people have the most personal freedoms that they could possibly have, without the interference of any other person or government. I hope that is something that most of us can agree on. Now let me pose the second part of this … If anyone could do anything they wanted, that is, they had endless personal freedom wouldn't that mean that we would have complete chaos?

Oliver Wendell Homes once said, "Your liberty to swing your fist ends just where my nose begins." (Shapiro & Epstein, 2006) We all want to live with absolute freedom, but we cannot do that if it impacts another person. We would all be constantly breaking each other's noses if we didn't agree to some rules of engagement with each other; For example, driving into each other on highways, falling off uncompleted bridges, etc. Most of us understand that some government, therefore, however small, is required in order that we have some organization and control in the nature of keeping everyone safe. "The American Founders considered the two extremes to be anarchy on the one hand and tyranny on the other. At one extreme of anarchy there is no government, no law, no systematic control and no government power, while at the other extreme, there is too much control, (too much law) too much political oppression and too much government."(Skousen, 1981, p. 10) The object of the Founders was to discover the "balanced center" between these two extremes." It took many years for the founders of our country to derive a system that could balance these opposite ideas and interests.

Now, about the two-party system. The 13 colonies became independent from England's control in 1776 but as previously pointed out, America would not form a single nation for 11 years after. The Articles of Confederation were written in 1777 to provide structure for elected officials to meet together from the states and discuss various issues that existed between them. At some point, it was decided to embark on the forming of a wholly new type of government that would be run by the people, for the people. Early on in this experiment, it became apparent that we needed a central taxing authority to pay for the War (against Mother England) and to protect the lands to the West of the colonies. A primary task was to decide how much to tax the states. Alexander Hamilton was our first national Treasury secretary responsible for setting up a system of taxation. Thomas Jefferson, representative of Virginia, sought to place limits on the power of our federal government. This was the beginning of the two-party system. Hamilton's party became known as the Federalists, who generally speaking, tilted toward providing the Federal government with the size and power it needed to keep the peace, organize the states' affairs, erect borders, enact international trade rules, etc. Jefferson's party became known as the Republicans, whose primary concerns and interests were in limiting federal power as much as possible, to keep control with the individual states, and that of the individual landowners. Our founders relied on the two-party system to balance these fair yet competing interests. Today, the party of Hamilton is called the Democratic Party, and the party of Jefferson is still called the Republican Party. The parties still exist, and represent the two main counterbalancing schools of thought. You will figure out if the two-party system is important moving forward -it may or may not be. That is up to you to decide. What is most important is that we first relearn the original intent behind the system. The two parties were not meant to be used to oppose each other, rather to respectfully check the other to achieve balance.

The founders were very aware of the potential for *radical*[148] or fringe players in each of the parties. They talked about the dangers of extreme positions often.

Now, I am going to attempt to describe how these two very different sides think and act. First some ground rules: As you are reading my descriptions please don't jump to conclusions whether I believe that one camp is more right than the other. I've been trying to disguise my political identity, and I think it may be fun for you to later guess if there is a side I lean toward... Most of us do- naturally lean one way or the other and that is ok. If we can get to a point where we can poke a little fun at one another, that will be a really positive thing. Therefore, I am going to have some fun with my descriptions, even *stereotype*[149] a bit, painting a picture of the worst (most extreme) in either direction. It truly does not matter, for the purposes of this book, which side you may be on. As I've already said, there is only wrong on the extreme of each *ideology*[150]

Lastly, I don't want you to buy into any idea that there are overly powerful interest groups plotting to tear down our country. There is not some group of people sitting in a fancy hotel boardroom, or in some underground bunker somewhere *conspiring*[151] to ruin our lives. No matter what you hear from your parents, or grandparents -or your crazy Uncle Donny or Aunt Delores, or your friends- it does not work like this. Therefore, please clear your head of what you have been told, about the far left and far right. I ask you to notice instead how the differences between the two sides haven't changed much. Over the years a leftist talks and debates like a leftist and and rightist talks and debates like a rightist. We transfer administrations from one extreme to the other, decade after decade only to wind up at the same place- greatly divided. Watching a presidential debate today is like watching a re-run debate from thirty or forty years ago, but with

---

148. radical: especially of change or action) relating to or affecting the fundamental nature of something; far-reaching or thorough
149. stereotype: a widely held but fixed and oversimplified image or idea of a particular type of person or thing.
150. Ideaology: a system of ideas and ideals, especially one which forms the basis of economic or political theory and policy.
151. conspire: make secret plans jointly to commit an unlawful or harmful act.

different actors- same EXACT script. I do hope that you conclude, as I have, that there is something very weird and troubling about this.

Lastly, please pay special attention to the terminology of ``Wokism" and "Masculinity." They may be a little less familiar to you than the terms Democrat and Republican, and they are very important. So here we go:

First meet Sally, who represents the political LEFT. Sally is a proud liberal and a registered Democrat. She is generally for a bigger government not smaller. She sees the role of government to be primarily concerned with equalizing life experience, and having compassion for those in need. She is therefore supportive of a forced re-distribution of wealth through taxation to ensure this equalization process. She believes that the strong should be forced to help the weak. The faster help the slower. She tends to watch liberal news channels such as CNN and she listens to Public Radio. She believes that people are vulnerable enough to need strong local, state, and federal governments. She doesn't like violence. Sally rides a bicycle to and from work with a helmet on, and would never get on a motorcycle. She prefers fly fishing and fishes with old-fashioned fly rods. She always throws the baby fish back- because she doesn't want to hurt them, and to ensure that she doesn't harm the ecosystem. Sally does not like the fact that there is a first-class section on Delta Airlines, and she generally assumes that the people sitting there did not earn it. The fact that Disney World sells a pass for $400 dollars that allows people to cut the line, turns Sally's stomach. She would rather wait in the two-hour line for Space Mountain, with everyone else. Sally is a sailor, she drives slowly, obeys the rules, eats cheese, and sips wine. She saves the whales whenever she can. She is generally known by others for having compassion- and it's real. Sally believes that climate change is a scientific fact and that humans are causing it. She therefore drives an electric vehicle like a Ford Fusion, with a peace sticker on it. Sally supports any movement which is for equal rights and opportunities for any kind of living organism, no matter where they live or where they came from. Sally might appreciate being called a *Xenophilia*[152]- a person who has *"an affection for*

---

152. Xenophilia: an affection for unknown/foreign objects, manners, culture and people

unknown/foreign objects, manners, culture, and people."

Our Sallys these days tend to be younger. They are likely to be thinking and saying "I need to be seen because I matter", "be awake to my needs," "See me," "Hear me," Sallys tend to see the proper role of government to provide not only equal opportunities but equal things. They see results, and people's positions in life, (such as poverty, skin color) as strong evidence that a political process or policy is broken. They tend to be our coddlers. They tend to be apologetic and see an admission to mistakes as a sign of intelligence and strength rather than weakness. Last but not least, our Sally's tend to be our overthinkers, rather than our underthinkers.

Now let's meet Bob, who represents the typical person on the political RIGHT. Bob is a "Conservative" who votes Republican. Bob believes in a smaller government not bigger. He believes that the government should Tax people as little as possible, and that any redistribution of money or wealth through forced taxation is *blasphemy[153]*. The strong beat the weak. The fast beat the slow. Bob watches conservative news stations such as FOX. He isn't aware of Public Radio. Bob wants to be left alone with little to no government interference. He thinks that people are smart enough to be left to figure stuff out on their own. That we should fight for our lives and let the chips fall where they may. "Wild Wild West Baby". Bob doesn't mind a fight and thinks it's good for us once in a while. Bob rides a big fat motorcycle without a helmet, and wouldn't be caught dead riding a bicycle. When Bob fishes he does so with auto reels and electric nets. He kills what he catches and eats it, if a few babies are eaten that's ok too- they can't all be "keepers." Bob loves the fact that there is a first-class section on Delta Airlines and generally assumes the people sitting there earned it. The fact that Disney sells a pass for $400 dollars that allows people to cut the line makes Bob really happy, especially when he has one in his pocket. Bob arrogantly sprints by people who are waiting in the 3-hour line for Space Mountain while waving his speed pass over his head proudly. Bob is a powerboater, drives fast, breaks the rules, eats steak, drinks hard alcohol in the form of Martini's or shots, and also chugs beer. He hunts and kills the whales when he sees one.

---

153. blasphemy: the act or offense of speaking sacrilegiously about God or sacred things; profane talk

Bob is not known for his compassion- but tends to claim it as a real strength (when it's really not). He doesn't care too much about climate change, or if people are responsible for it. If the earth should begin to burn, Bob figures that he will put the fire out himself. Bob drives a Hummer Pick Up Truck with a bumper sticker that says "suck it up." Bob would not mind being called a *xenophobe*[154]- *" a person having a dislike of or prejudice against people from other countries"*.

Our Bobs these days tend to be older. They are likely to be thinking and saying "just leave me alone" or "You think you are smarter than I am, well let me tell you something". They see the proper role of government as to provide equal opportunity but not equal things. They don't necessarily see the results, or people's situation (such as poverty or skin color, or upbringing) as evidence to change policy or process. They tend to believe in tough love. They tend to be unapologetic. They think that admitting a mistake is a sign of weakness and that America as a government should not spend time apologizing for itself. Last but not least, they tend to be our underthinkers, rather than our overthinkers.

If I've offended any Bobs or Sallys with these descriptions please keep in mind that it is my opinion that in its extreme form, one is no worse than the other.

While trying to remain neutral please think of the term "woke" as being similar in meaning to the terms enlightened, or awakened. Please also take as a fact that wokism is an outgrowth of the prefrontal cortex in our brain, so we will call these people our "prefrontals", or "frontal lobes". Please also accept that masculinity is exclusively an outgrowth of the brain stem. Therefore, you may hear me refer to them simply- as our Brain Stems. For the sake of further discussion, please take it that our "Progressives" are mostly our frontal lobes. A progressive generally seeks progress, questions everything and is overly quick to act. "Preservationists" are your brain stems. They seek to preserve the past, question very little and if there is to be change they like to see it happen slowly.

Therefore, in summary: we have our ultra wokes v ultra

---

154. xenophobe: a person having a dislike of or prejudice against people from other countries

masculines, prefrontals v brain stems, progressives v. preservationists, overthinkers v. underthinkers, liberal v. conservative, democrat v republican, left vs. right.

SALLY vs.	BOB
Ultra-Woke	Ultra-Masculine
Prefrontals	Brain Stems
Progressives	Preservationists
Over Thinkers	Under Thinkers
Liberal	Conservative
Democrat	Republican
Left	Right

Please see my Sally V. Bob chart. If you have not already noticed, these two types of people are so different that they may as well come from different planets. Now add back in everything you've learned about human beings from Cicero and Dr. Haidt. With this background, let's now consider the sequence of events that caused these two opposite thinkers to come crashing into each other in brand new ways, to create the absolute shit storm of abnormality we have been living in: Sound like fun? Here goes:

In January of 2009 Barack Obama, a Democrat, became our 44th President, replacing a Republican, George W. Bush. The liberal left was understandably happy and many overthinkers were even gloating a bit. Progressive groups such as LGBTQIA+ began to organize quickly and expand rapidly. Let's just say it was a good time to be a fly fisherman or to wear a pink bow tie! Meanwhile, republicans were generally concerned, and the far-right preservationists sitting on their gas-guzzling powerboats soothing their brain stems and drowning their sorrows with Vodka Martinis and cold beers. However, they would not take defeat lightly. Within days of the inauguration, our masculines shook off their hangovers and mobilized a counter-offensive attack called the American Tea Party Movement.

At this time, Facebook had reached 500 Million users in the four short years since its founding. Americans were new to receiving messages in highly misleading, emotionally charged, and often untrue, bite-sized pieces. The image quality of the messaging had improved as well. Have you ever seen that TV commercial when someone drops an egg on a hot skillet and the voice says "This is your Brain on Drugs" as the egg sizzles. Or the Quit Smoking commercial with the lady with no toes and tubes sticking out of her neck? The Tea Party and its supporters in right-wing news channels, led by Fox News utilized this new type of sensationalized messaging to foretell a dark story about a dangerously ballooning federal government. The message: Programs for the "underserved," "underprivileged," "underrepresented," "disenfranchised" or "marginalized" would grow quickly. Government would become so enormous that we would have to increase taxes to construct new federal buildings across the country to house more federal employees. If not stopped, our newly elected liberal president, and his like-minded clan of ultra-wokes, would turn our system into something called Socialism. Under this system, the government would increase taxes and redistribute wealth, as they saw fit because the government knows better than we do. "They" would equalize everything and wouldn't stop until the job was done. If you had a boat in your backyard, look out the government was coming for it. Restaurants would be forced to serve free food every day at a fixed time for lunch, the same type of shitty soup, or a plate of disgusting meatballs, every day- would lack quality because it was free. Incentives for creativity and innovation would stop. We would all soon grow dependent on the government. Meanwhile, facts or details to support any of this would not enter into the minds of any of us birdbrains...

For eight years, while young Obama was in office the preservationist right remained busy with their media campaign. They even gave big government a big scary name- The Deep Blue State. Our federal government became known as a swamp.

A dirty rotten cesspool inhabited by dirty politicians who were liars and cheats. "Career politicians," they said were only serving for the kickbacks and favors and feeling of power received from their constituents, (friends, family, lobbyists). The image of the deep blue state struck an open nerve with people because, as I earlier indicated, most people have a natural dislike for authority and government to begin with. I want to believe that the people in the Tea Party and who were placing all these negative ads together did not know of the long-term impact that they would have. I want to believe that they lack awareness of how susceptible human beings are to fear campaigns. I want to believe that they did not play on our fears intentionally.

Regardless of my wishful thinking, the damage had been done. The messaging about the dangers of big government was the most successful *propaganda*[155] campaign in the history of our country. It changed everything. Disliking the government and thinking poorly of our politicians became as American as apple pie and Chevrolet. If any citizen is asked what they think about politicians today, they automatically go with the popular answer. I don't even have to tell you, because you know what the answer is, it is deeply ingrained in the American psyche, but an image of a catfish or a scum-sucking bottom dweller might come to mind?

Now- enter Hillary Clinton and The Donald into the next Presidential election cycle. If you tried for another million years, you could not create a person in Hillary Clinton that fit the description of a liberal democrat of the type I described. Hillary stood for everything that an excessively feminine, apologetic, compassionate, and overthinking person could amount to. Hillary, according to greatly exaggerated media branding by the far right, would make my Sally look like a Bud Light drinker! On the other hand, you could search the universe and never find a person who more accurately fits my description of a conservative Republican than Donald Trump. The Donald stood for everything that a masculine, unapologetic, uncompassionate, and underthinking person could stand for. The Donald, according to his greatly exaggerated media branding by the far left, would tell my Bob to grow a pair!

---

155. propaganda: information, especially of a biased or misleading nature, used to promote or publicize a particular political cause or point of view.

Hillary and The Donald became larger-than-life *caricatures*[156] which embodied all of the worst features of their respective political ideology. Every American voter had become hard-wired to think if elected each would excessively serve their own base, rather than serve all Americans. Each side started to believe that the other side was rotten to the core. The 2016 election would leave the American voters with a choice between two evils of greatly exaggerated identity. You are old enough to know the rest of the story. The Donald won. Martinis would fly on every motorboat from coast to coast. The Democrats would be the ones with the hangovers this time. They huddled on their sailboats and uncharacteristically guzzled wine (it was organic...) from the bottle, fearing for the next four years of "Uncle Donny" leadership.

Conservative America had just dealt the Democrats a mighty blow. What our Sallys decided to do next would be the final straw and have historical significance. Just when we thought things couldn't get any worse, there would be one final mistake, in the form of an unintended albeit self-inflicted knockout punch.

Desperate of losing the progress they thought they had made for people they thought needed the protection of the Federal government most, the extreme liberal left decided that they needed to teach everyone a few things. In an effort to retain what they thought they would lose under a Trump administration, (in social policy, progressive thinking, and awareness) they went to corporate America and begged them to get involved. Corporate America listened and went to the airwaves to try to teach everyone a bunch of things- about fairness, race relations, diversity, equity, and inclusion. **Things that we already knew**. This move resulted in the final *plagues*[157] which would soon befall upon the American people- **Political correctness, and Phoniness.**

Let me give you an example of "new normal" phoniness.

---

156. caricature: a picture, description, or imitation of a person in which certain striking characteristics are exaggerated in order to create a comic or grotesque effect
157. plague: a contagious bacterial disease characterized by fever and delirium,

Recently, I was watching a college basketball game on a national station and a commercial came on. It started with a kid in his bedroom, it looked like a teenager, with an up-close shot of his open mouth, he had a slight mustache and a huge gap between his two front teeth. It looked like a boy although he was wearing lipstick... he flung on a bright yellow coat and bounded down the stairs into the living room, where his mom (a black lady) and dad (Asian guy), were at the kitchen table with other kids, maybe siblings, but all of different color skin, brown, black, white etc. The camera then pans to a dog (a fluffy golden) with a bandage on his leg and it looks like he is in a wheelchair. The dog that is, in a wheelchair. The kid ends up at school, passing a very large and sweaty woman (over 400 lbs I would estimate) who was clearly exercising on his way in. The kid does a twirl in front of the class, takes his seat and the music ends. Before it ends the advertiser warns me that whatever it was selling could cause me vomiting, nausea, and diarrhea, and when it was all over I didn't even know what the Ad was for. In fact, I've since seen the commercial four or five more times, and I still can't tell you what it's trying to sell me.

You know what phoniness looks like, us humans can smell it from a mile away. Phoniness is in the same camp as trying too hard or forcing things. When someone is trying too hard, we can feel the awkwardness. It's worse when we are being lied to, or spoken down too. Most people have the common sense to know when they are being bullshitted. Phoniness not only offends our common sense, (which riles up the emotional elephant in us) but it does something worse than that. It opens another door in our minds. It escalates our preexisting irrational fears and leads to more extreme thoughts and overreactions. It makes us think the worst about what people are capable of. A few examples to make this point.

A few years ago, I was involved in the Little League in my town. You remember Oliver and the gang! In my last few years, there was a movement by parents in my town to stop keeping score in our youngest division called the farm league, ages ten and eleven. The town next to us had stopped keeping score and was giving Trophies to both teams following tournament play. That is, the winners and the losers, in case you weren't paying attention. Because Little League baseball is a taxpayer-supported activity, there was quite a disturbance in our town, between the two types of political thinkers. Sally was proud to give little Oliver, who struck out three times and dropped a fly ball, a Trophy, I guess for helping his team lose. Bob was beside himself- he wanted to strangle poor little Oliver. I was on the board of baseball at that time. It wasn't a paid gig and I remember it being one of the hardest things I've ever had to deal with. Without giving away which side I leaned on, all I can say is that the idea of several Martinis and a few shots was looking pretty good...

Last summer, while on the beach with my family and a group of friends, the conversation turned to gender pronouns. The whole non-binary, he/ she or they issue. My 14-year-old nephew and his friends got up and left immediately, with one of the youngest kids telling his mother, "Mom my stomach hurts when I talk about this stuff." I was saddened to see that it had come to this. I had become familiar with the issue of boys who were transitioning their sex to female, and vice versa. One case was in the news where apparently a boy who was in the process of transitioning to a girl, was competing and winning swim races, at a public university. So people were in an uproar about it, it was on the TV nightly. Around this same time, a news story broke about a school in Arizona that was considering placing kitty litter in the school's bathroom to accommodate a request by certain middle school-age kids who were claiming to identify as animals. They apparently wanted to enforce their individual preference to pee on the ground into a kitty litter box instead of the facilities more traditionally provided. This issue of Animal pronouns was new to me, and I must admit it took me a few minutes to understand it, or if someone was pulling my leg. So I began to do some research and According to the LBGTQIA+ Wiki "Catgender is also described as someone who strongly identifies with cats or other felines or experiences delusions relating to being a cat or feline." The issues of gender fluidity, and animal pronouns are complex. If you think I'm sounding insensitive please just give me a few more seconds to explain myself.

In May of 2022, news broke of a rather widespread movement to change the name of Mother's Day to "National Birthing Persons Day," apparently out of respect for people who take offense to the term "mother." Fox News reported that President Biden was seriously considering ending Mother's Day. However, that turned out to be a lie. The President quickly came on the TV to defend Mother's Day. However, the topic engineered by a few people who wanted to change Mothers aDy to Birthing Persons Day would remain in the news for months. It was utilized by every staunch republican in the land, to reinforce the dangers of the democratic party. Even Though there was never any truth to the rumor. Millions of people believed the lie and would come to be certain that the old-timer, Biden, had lost his marbles enough to cancel Mother's Day. So back to the TV commercial I was telling you about earlier.

After my fifth or sixth viewing, I finally figured out that it was for a vacuum cleaner. I don't know about you, but I don't need a vacuum manufacturer telling me that I need to be more compassionate for my dog. I love my dog. The company should tell me how its vacuum works and why I should choose it over other vacuums. Does it suck harder? Does it have longer battery life? The company shouldn't be spending its time worrying about whether I am a good person. I may not be a good person, but be honest- You just want me to buy your damn vacuum right? It offends my sensibilities. Also, I am all about diversity- so corporate America doesn't need to keep shoving it in my face. It's fine to celebrate diversity, equity, and inclusion in America, and nobody has a problem with that, because most of us already have a strong sense of fairness and compassion. Only a very small percentage of us actually lose our compassion along the journey of life. I feel badly for both those groups who feel that they have been marginalized or mistreated in the past and those who have actually been. I look forward to speaking about these issues in the community at community events, and in school. I don't need Gatorade, or Amazon, or Lululemon to tell me that overweight people exercise, I know that. Or that they deserve to drink Gatorade, I know that too. Or that the $150 dollar spandex tights come in quadruple XXXX. I already assumed that 400-pound women of any color could shop there too.

I have more range than you give me credit for. I already feel more than you do, I am a person, you are a TV set, and when you talk down to me, I turn you off. 99% of young adults feel the same way. Even our Ostriches with their heads in the sand can see through this crap. We can all feel phoniness, and it causes us to distrust each other even more than we already do. When corporations or governments push these things on us, it has a negative unintended consequence. Please stop. The TV should be for entertainment. We need to turn off the political messaging. We need to do away with the word politics altogether and replace it with civics. People are not going to celebrate diversity because we tell them to. They are going to celebrate diversity only because they have a value system that believes in these things.

Everywhere I look in my Town there are lawn signs telling me to "Stop Asian hate" and that Black Lives Matter. There is nobody in the world, I believe, who wants to stop any form of hate other than me. I truly appreciate the sentiment, to Stop Asian Hate; and that Black Lives Matter. I know that I am treading on a fine line here, and I want to be careful, because being more careful about what we say, is in large part a major theme of this book. I understand that people who push for these slogans believe that they were pushed into a corner and have no choice to respond in an aggressive way and push back against the system. But we are the system. At some point, as activists, we need to realize that our trying too hard, and forcing things is backfiring on us. While the signs don't bother me, that isn't the point. There are just too many of them!!! I don't need to be told not to hate Asian people, because I have no hate or disregard for Asian people, regardless of what any moron might tell me about the Coronavirus starting in China. Over 90% of us know that people who have a dislike for Chinese people because of Covid 19 are wrong. By paying too much attention to the fringe element, the extremists on both sides, we call attention to them and unknowingly keep them relevant, and we allow a small percentage of our society to define what we think of each other.

Some of the ideas, like kitty litter, being proposed by the progressive left are startling at first. I think it would take 371 Million moderate and modest philosophers to meet in person while getting back rubs and sipping hot chocolate with marshmallows, (or wine for democrats and beers and shots for republicans) to successfully work out all the complexities of childhood gender fluidity, dysmorphia and animal pronouns. I mean this is hard stuff! We want to respect people who are going through it, but we also want to respect people who don't want to see our social policy, and societal norms shaped by it. There are truly good people on both sides of all the issues. Most people don't harbor any ill will toward other people, Asian, black, transgender, or otherwise. I know many people don't think this is true. I believe it is true of young people.

In order for me to make my final point, it's important for you to know that not all fear of big government is unwarranted. From a Tax perspective, the fear of an overly large government can be very real. I want to give you a quick example from my life. I sold my business in 2021 and paid more federal taxes in one year than I had ever before. I'm proud and happy to have paid the taxes that I did. But let me make my point with a hypothetical; If I sold the business for 5 Million and paid $30 percent tax that would be $ 1.5 million of the $5 Million. Under a socialist government, my taxes could have been as high as 60%. Can you imagine selling a business that you worked very hard at to build for almost thirty years and then having to pay the government $3 MILLION of the $ 5 million? That is not far off our current reality. Now for the summary conclusion of the play-by-play.

Before he was elected, Mr. Trump told a reporter on a national TV show that he could "grab women by the Vaginas," he could "do it whenever" he wants, and that they "they loved it." He called Mexicans wet and dirty. He called John McCain, an American war hero, a loser. He called liberal women ugly and disgusting and made overweight people feel badly about themselves. Knowing all this, millions of educated adults still voted for him. Why?

Because they were scared. Scared that if the party of Hillary and Sally won, that there would be no more scoring in baseball, no more Mother's Day and kitty litter boxes would be installed in all of our schools for kids who identify as furries. If we had a President who would support a boy with a penis competing in girls swim races, what would stop them from raising taxes to 60%? I don't mean to offend anyone, and I am not trying to be funny. Voters were driven by emotive fears, the same exact ones that each of us feel when giving a speech.

Today, we have these two sides coming at each other, who are scared of each other and who have stopped listening to each other. On the liberal left, we have people who have yet learned how to like Roman emperors, coming across with a sense of entitlement, talking over credible adults, gettin' in people's faces, ready to pounce on the establishment for any abbreviation however small of their misunderstood entitlements. They are offended by everything when they aren't even old enough to have been victimized to the extent that they complain of. If you have become one of these people, you may think that you are free to behave like victims when you are not yet victims or to demand that your concerns about peeing in kitty litter boxes be heard the same day, but according to reality (natural law) you are not free to behave in this way. You may think that you are free to make your demands with protests that include illegal interruptions, violence, and looting, but you are not. This type of expression is not working for you. It's radical, it's extreme, it will not work. Because it's unnatural you are causing 50% of the Country to tune you out. I would ask these young people to realize that they are pushing too hard, and doing more damage to your causes than they have been able to realize. You have been tuned out and cast aside as an out-of-touch angry "woke" mob.

On the other side, on the extreme right, we have conservatives who are not thinking like Roman emperors, who think that they are free to tune people out completely, because they look different, or because they are of a different race, color, or gender. But here is the thing, Bob ... You do not get to independently decide who or what is normal in this world. You may think you are free to say that liberal politicians are turning our country into a dirty pile of cow shit because college-educated people are considering issues surrounding slavery and its lingering, systemic effects, or when you load undocumented refugee families seeking asylum in your state onto buses in the middle of the night to other states without notification- you are not free to do these things. The natural laws will catch up with you. You will lose in the end. Your unapologetic arrogance is not a demonstration of American freedom, and by being so arrogant 50% of the people are NOT listening to you. They have cast you aside as irrelevant and stupid.

People on the other side of your political viewpoint are not the only ones missing the point. You are all missing the point. Regardless of what extreme side you are on -you may all think that you are winning your fight, but you are not. You are all stuck in second gear, and spinning your wheels. You are hurting those people who you are intending to help. You are losing your war and wasting your time.The shortsightedness in our approach is not working consistent with violation of NL 101, our failure to self-master, and this is having a disproportionate impact on the rest of society consistent with NL 102.

We need to understand that with every unthinking word, we are triggering the other side, into overreaction. We may not think that our opinion is extreme enough to trigger the other side, but it does.

I'm not asking any activist on either side to give up your fight. We can all continue to fight for what we believe is right, I'm just asking that everyone consider a different way of getting there. It doesn't do anyone any good to think that we are right, or even to know that we are right if we can't get the other side to agree with us. My father used to say to me "Glenn it's not what you say, it's how you say it." Most often it's only a matter of HOW we present our opinions that are offending people. You will only win over peoples minds when you can state your opponent's viewpoint, as well as your own. The key for us younger folks (I better complete this book soon...) is for each side to learn how to speak the other side's language; to go into political discussions with our worldview (or ideology) being the opposite of what we think.

As promised, I will end this chapter with a few more absolute statements of truth. The reality is that there is no right or wrong, being conservative or liberal, or being a Democrat or Republican. The problem is not being woke, it's being too woke. The problem is not being masculine, it's being too masculine. I honestly do not know what is worse, a Trophy for Oliver, or a repeat performance by our Uncle Donny as President… but what I do know for certain is that either extreme will keep us divided forever.

We have two types of people, left siders and right siders. Overthinkers and underthinkers. Their personalities and preferences track perfectly to the left and right side of our brains. These two sides envision each other as greatly exaggerated enemies, and these statements are all supported by science. I mean C'mon Mr. Postmodernist, with all this evidence will you still not agree that extremism on both sides is causing our problems? Or do you still think that you are free to think and do whatever you want? Please look around you. We have been making the same mistakes for over 2000 years. Please accept natural law as truth and the only authority we need. How many people will literally have to die before we will fully listen and change? Will our hitting rock bottom finally do the trick? I'm counting on it.

Chapter 9: The New Normal

We finally made it- to the new normal. I've never been more excited to talk about something that resembles a virus, because this is the turning point. We begin our road back here. Our new normal is what provided me with the justification for spending the last few years of my life in the library, and driving my wife crazy, while searching for some reliable sources of truth. This chapter is dedicated to providing the last bit of proof for the existence of the Natural Laws. The best proof they say is always "in the pudding". The results never lie.

I cannot think of anyone more appropriate to lead us off in describing our new normal than Dr. Haidt, who has inspired me with knowledge, as a philosopher and scientist. He tells a story from the Bible of a great society whose people were so united, they built a tower so tall that it nearly touched the heavens. According to the tale, he writes "God was offended by the *hubris*[158]- of mankind and said, "Look, they are ONE people, and they have ONE language, and this is only the beginning of what they will do; nothing they propose to do will now be impossible for them. Come, let us go down, and confuse their language there, so that they will not understand one another's speech." The Bible does not conclude whether God destroyed the tower but Dr. Haidt asks his readers to "hold that dramatic image in our minds; people wandering amid the ruins, unable to communicate, condemned to mutual incomprehension." He writes "The story of Babel is the best metaphor I could come up with for the fractured country we now inhabit. Something went terribly wrong, very suddenly. We are disoriented, unable to speak the same language or recognize the same truth. We are cut off from one another and the past. It has been clear for quite a while now that red America and blue America are like two different countries...with two different versions of the Constitution, economics, and American history. It's about the shattering of all that had seemed solid, the scattering of people who had been a community." (Haidt, 2022)

According to an article in Newsweek magazine, The Anxiety Pandemic, Dan Hurley, the number of adults reporting

---

158. hubris: excessive pride or self-confidence

depression and anxiety has "jumped to 41 percent in 2021, from 11 percent in 2019"- "Anxiety has become so widespread... that in September, '22a US Task Force... recommended that adults under the age of 65 get screened for the condition." (Hurley, 2022). In 2021, adolescents in the U.S. between the age of 12 to 17 experienced at least one major depressive episode, representing 14.7% of the population within the age group. (*Major Depression*, n.d.-b) Americans' blood pressure is up, and measures of mental health are down. Alcohol abuse and drug overdoses are at all-time highs, as of March of 2020. (Hanson, 2023) Even vehicle crashes have surged. The number of "doomsday preppers," that is the number of people who think that we are all doomed and society is coming to an end during their lifetimes, has spiked in the last several years, from what was roughly 2% of the population to upwards of 10%! (CBS News, 2022) Sadly, this increase is not due to the rise in tornadoes...

"Nearly 80 percent are dissatisfied with the country's direction, according to Gallup." "America suffers from societal and political conditions that predispose it to violence," says Michael Jenkins, in an article he wrote for RAND, dated 2021. Politics "now manifests itself in the demonization of political opponents as primal enemies- tyrants, traitors, terrorists. Polarization has... contributed to the loss of *comity*[159] in political discourse which has turned crude insults, *ad hominem*[160] attacks, and the notion that profanity displays authenticity. Political rhetoric is seemingly intended to inflame passions, at times bordering on criminal incitement. Some news channels and the internet (along with foreign influence...) stoke the differences, and facts are often irrelevant. This uncivil culture makes vicious attacks and harassment of public officials common, discouraging ordinary people from entering public service, while attracting *zealots*[161]. *Irreconcilable*[162] differences on social issues reinforce the

---

159. comity: courtesy and considerate behavior toward others
160. ad hominem: (of an argument or reaction) directed against a person rather than the position they are maintaining
161. zealot: a person who is fanatical and uncompromising in pursuit of their religious, political, or other ideals.
162. irreconcilable: (of ideas, facts, or statements) representing findings or points of view that are so different from each other that they cannot be made compatible.

political divide. Differences over racial injustice, abortion, gun control, immigration, and LGBTQIA+ rights increasingly determine whom one is willing to associate with, reinforcing self-segregation along political lines as a group with like-minded friends and partners." Mr. Jenkins says, "Americans do fewer things together. Church attendance is declining. Membership in civic organizations and lodges has been decreasing for decades. Parent Teacher Association (PTA) membership has dropped by nearly half of what it was in the 1960s. Bowling leagues have almost disappeared... Meanwhile, self-proclaimed citizen *militias*[163] are held together by their shared hatred of the federal government." ..."Americans don't even have a sense of a shared history. Is America's story one of a moral crusade dedicated to defending the inalienable rights of life, liberty, and the pursuit of happiness of which we should be proud? Or is it a story of territorial expansion, slaughter, slavery, and *imperialism*[164] of which it should be ashamed? (Jenkins, 2021)

"When citizens lose trust in elected leaders, health authorities, the courts, the police, universities, and the integrity of elections, then every decision becomes contested; every election becomes a life and death struggle to save the country from the other side. "(Haidt, 2022, p. 12) Alan Fuer, Boston Globe "When political aggression is set in the context of a war... people with no prior history are more likely to accept it. Political violence can also be made more palatable by couching it as a defensive action against a belligerent enemy. That is particularly true if an adversary is persistently described as irredeemably evil or less than human." Fuer gives an example, Kari Lake, Republican nominee for Governor of Arizona 2022, speaking at a large event in Dallas in 2022 said, "Our Government is rotten to the core... This is truly a battle between those who want to save America and those who want to destroy her... If we accept it, America is dead. My question to you is: Are you in this fight with us?" -Jeff Jacoby, Boston Globe writes, "The heightened use of *bellicose*[165],

---

163. militia: a military force that is raised from the civil population to supplement a regular army in an emergency
164. imperialism: a policy of extending a country's power and influence through diplomacy or military force
165. bellicose: demonstrating aggression and willingness to fight.

dehumanizing and *apocalyptic*[166] language, particularly by prominent figures... is causing violence to happen. We have all but forgotten how to reason, how to compromise, how to keep disagreement from devolving into *enmity*[167]... (Jacoby, 2022)

People perceive their political opponents not as people with a different point of view, but as actual physical enemies. Fuer writes, "Threats of political violence and actual attacks have become a steady reality of American life, affecting school board officials, election workers, flight attendants, librarians and even members of congress, with few headlines and very little reaction from politicians."

The ADL's Center on Extremism "is charged with tracking all forms of extremism and hate online and in the real world... Oren Segal notes that " a profound cultural shift has taken place over the course of a generation. Whereas once conspiracy theories and extremist movements marked by antisemitism, racism and other hateful ideas were a somewhat obscure issue, now they're easy to access and readily available, making it more likely that people will fall under their sway." (Greenblatt, 2022, p. 31)

ADL Exec VP Oren Segal writes, "there was a reason the Klan wore masks, because they weren't accepted by society." Today, haters don't have to wear masks. Somehow, it's become ok, even normal or acceptable. "radicals on both sides of the ideological spectrum perceive that there's nothing wrong with what they are doing, and they feel like they're being accepted. They sense that they have strength in numbers so long as they stay together." (Greenblatt, 2022, p. 29) Hate has become a daily part of our lives. "Haters have not only been tolerated by politicians on both sides of the political spectrum, they have been encouraged by people at the highest levels of our government."(Greenblatt, 2022, p. 27) Haters are more *emboldened*[168] than they have ever been, as they have been empowered by certain politicians and public figures who lend them either direct support, or who fail to

---

166. apocalyptic: describing or prophesying the complete destruction of the world.

167. enmity: the state or feeling of being actively opposed or hostile to someone or something

168. embolden: give (someone) the courage or confidence to do something or to behave in a certain way

denounce their hateful rhetoric. (Greenblatt, 2022, pp. 27–29)

"Violent extremist groups' activity is one thing, but we're also besieged by a broader wave of hateful speech and ideology that is infiltrating American Culture and daily life." "A toxic combination of social media and *demagoguery*[169] is to blame. Segal speaks of "social media phenomenon where we all create our world view through the information we consume and where conspiracy theories and disinformation are as *ubiquitous*[170] as legitimate news." The result is a subtle but pervasive normalization of hate, made worse by political leaders who disseminate ideas that were formerly beyond the pale, affirming their validity, or who remain silent, giving others an excuse not to step up and correct the hateful rhetoric." "Extremist *agitators*[171] *exploit*[172] the opening provided by social media, manipulating messaging to change minds and win new *adherents*[173]." They make hate more attractive to younger audiences by clothing it in ironic humor or imbedding it in youth culture. The ADL reports "teens posting images on social media of their Jewish classmates in ovens" denoting a wish to see them die, and "students bullying immigrant children saying to them "we are going to build a wall" to keep you out of America. "America is a society saturated in hate." (Greenblatt, 2022, pp. 27–33) The FBI reported more hate crimes in America in 2020 than in any of the prior 12 years. The bottom line, "Our culture is fraying at the seams, and it wont knit itself back together."(Jacoby, 2022)

According to the Boston Globe, "Since February of 2018, when 34 students and teachers were shot, 17 fatally at Marjory Stoneman High School in Parkland Fl. There have been at least **2,741** mass shootings- (a mass shooting is defined where more than 4 people are killed) with over 40 more since Jan 1 (2023)…

---

169. demagoguery: political activity or practices that seek support by appealing to the desires and prejudices of ordinary people rather than by using rational argument
170. ubiquitous: present, appearing, or found everywhere.
171. agitators: a person who urges others to protest or rebel.
172. exploit: make full use of and make derive benifit from (a resource)
173. adherent: someone who supports a particular party, person, or set of ideas.

Gun violence is now the leading cause of death for children ages 1-19 in America. Every 30 minutes a child or teen is shot and every three hours a child or teen dies from gun violence. America is the gun violence capital of the developed world..."

There has been one mass murder* EVERY DAY SINCE 2014. There are so many mass shootings in America, to try to name them, would require its own book. Here are only **a** few examples from recent memory:

Buffalo NY, May 14, 2022, an 18-year-old white male walked into a Tops Supermarket with a semi-automatic rifle and shot and killed 10 innocent people. He live-streamed part of the attack on an internet social media site called Twitch. The killer was reported to have described himself as an *ethno-nationalist*[174] and a supporter of white supremacy who is motivated to commit political violence. He was active on social media prior to his rampage, voicing his support for *Great Replacement Theory*[175]. All victims were black.

El Paso, TX Aug 3, 2019, a mass shooting at a Walmart. 23 dead, all Latino, and targeted by the shooter because of his perceived hate for them. The shooter had been on the internet researching a conspiracy theory, called the Great Replacement Theory.

New Zealand, March 2019, 51 dead at church, the shooter, a white person who admitted he hates all non-white people.

Pittsburgh, PA October 27, 2108, a white man who hates Jewish people killed 11 in a synagogue, while they were praying. He posted a message online before the attack saying "jews like to bring invaders in that kill our people, I'm going in" Tree of Life Synagogue.

Orlando Florida, 2016, a man who admitted to hating Gay and

---

174. ethnonationalist: someone who believes nations are defined by common ancestry, language, and beliefs
175. Great Replacement Theory: a far-right conspiracy theory alleging that left-leaning domestic or international elites are attempting to replace white citizens with nonwhite (i.e., Black, Hispanic, Asian, or Arab) immigrants.

Lesbian people opened fire at a nightclub frequented by Gay and Lesbian people, killing 49 people.

Charleston SC, June 17, 2015, 21-year-old white man was invited into a church to pray, and instead opened fire on black churchgoers, killing nine. He spoke of his hate for black people in both a website manifesto published before the shooting and a journal which he wrote from jail afterward. On his website, he posted photos of emblems which are associated with white supremacy, including a photo of the Confederate battle flag.

Sutherland Springs TX, November 5, 2017, A man kills 26 people, in a church near San Antonio, including an unborn child, and wounded 22 others. He was bullied in school and became a misfit to all familiar with him.

Charlottesville, NC, August 12, 2017, admitted White Supremacist, deliberately drives his car into a crowd of people at a peaceful rally, killing one person and injuring 35. The offender had previously identified himself as neo nazi and white supremacist.

Las Vegas NV, October of 2017 -a deranged person shot more than 450 people killing 58 who were attending a music concert, shooting down from a hotel room from more than 2000 feet away, using military-style weapons and ammunition.

The mass murderers themselves are telling us that they are committing their crimes against society because they believe that more and more people support their actions.

It is beyond sad for me to think that one mass murder a day may seem normal to you. Or that it's become normal for you to have to worry about being shot and killed while at school. Your new normal has come to include **so** many things that are **so** far from normal. You are currently living through the worst violations of the natural laws that anyone has ever witnessed. It's on a *biblical*[176] scale. We have lost all semblance of who we are and who we were meant to be. It's as if we've become a whole new species. This is an indescribable place of intolerance, lack of understanding, and confusion that cuts against the grain of

---

176. biblical: very great; on a large scale

everything our forefathers once knew and for which our American system of law and government once stood for. If there is a God, and I think there is, he or she would be utterly devastated by what has unfolded on this earth.

What we are living through right now might best be described as a *perfect storm*[177]. Our perfect storm doesn't happen without some invisible elements. It's a combination of factors, led by poor leadership, which has come together in modern times to stunt our development. We should know better, but we are blind to many of the inputs. At the end of his second book, Dr. Haidt wrote, "This book explained why people are divided by politics and religion. The answer is not... because some people are good and some people are evil. Instead, the explanation is that our minds were designed for groupish righteousness. We are deeply intuitive creatures whose gut feelings drive our strategic reasoning. This makes it difficult- but not impossible- to connect with those who live in other matrices." (Haidt, 2013, p. 370) False fears and distortions of truth seep into our minds as *opaquely*[178] as the air we breathe due to pressures and hidden influences that we are NOT taught to understand.

We carry forward these false realities, or *myths*[179], while in our default mode unaware of their impact, and they create a nearly unbreakable cycle. I think about our cultural myths as the evil powder that we sprinkle in the washing machine while setting the DIAL to "Ordinary Man Approach- SPIN," but our making of myths is nothing to make light of. In fact, **our making light of myths, and our failing to understand how they are made, is in large part what keeps us tied to them.**

I don't like words that make my head hurt. Fascism is one of those words. However, "fascist politics" is a concept that is way too important for us not to know about, because it can help us understand how myths are created, in order that we can stop them. In his book, "How Fascism Works," author Jason Stanley explains, "Fascist politics seeks to undermine public discourse by attacking and devaluing education, expertise, and language.

---

177. perfect storm: a particularly bad or critical state of affairs, arising from a number of negative and unpredictable factors.
178. opaque: not able to be seen through; not transparent
179. myth: a widely held but false belief or idea

Intelligent debate is impossible without an education with access to different perspectives, a respect for expertise when one's own knowledge gives out, and a rich enough language to precisely describe reality. When education, expertise, and linguistic distinctions are undermined, there remains only power and tribal identity..." (Haidt, p. 36) A perfect storm and fascist politics are identical concepts.

There's an old saying I once heard that is very fitting to describe what is happening to us. "It's not the lions that eat us alive, it's the *gnats*[180]." Let me give you an example: We have come to accept as normal the practice of one politician putting another one down in order to try to earn our vote. The truth is that only the most cowardly and lowest form of human has to resort to pulling down the character of their rival to win. Politicians who have to resort to going negative on their opponents, rather than talking about what they would do as our leader, are not philosophers. They don't have the talent, the achievements, or the character to be a leader. A leader is someone who never misses an opportunity to cause all of us to awaken to the good in other people, by affirming the good in others. Instead of bringing out the best in us and showing us what we could be, our unqualified politicians cause us to doubt what we can be. They bring out the worst in us. This is what you've come to expect, and what you believe is normal. Well, it is not. Far from it- it's ruining our country and tearing down the potential you- as young Americans- have in your life. Please do not vote for people who run negative ads- They do not deserve your vote. Since you've been growing up, you've been witnessing the worst of what we have to offer, and us adults have allowed it to become your normal. I am sorry. I can't wait for you to see how things were truly meant to work.

It's time to bring our new normal to an end, however, it is not easy to fix something that we cannot see, or that we do not fully understand. Therefore, we have a little more work to do, to understand what I mean by invisible factors. We need to look at our myths in some detail to be sure that you can know how they are created- so that you can see through them. We may even

---

180. gnats: a small two-winged fly that resembles a mosquito. Gnats include both biting and non-biting forms, and they typically form large swarms

need to summon some higher powers to be able to deal with these invisible forces. But we've covered a lot of ground at this point. I want to take a well-deserved break, then we will return to finishing our work together.

Right now I have some great news that I've been wanting to share with you. We have many more reasons to be optimistic than just the shitty pudding itself. I want to use this next chapter to provide you a glimpse at a much brighter future.

Chapter 10: Breakthrough

How do you want to live your life? Choose from the below options

Column A:

For the most part you:

- Wake most days and believe it is a gift
- Feel good about yourself
- Don't worry too much about how others perceive you
- Have many rewarding and enjoyable friendships
- Feel healthy and have energy to explore the day
- Feel optimistic about your future
- Feel gratitude for the wonders of life
- Contribute to various things, and take pride in your contribution
- Look forward, not backward
- Understand that to have some regrets and sadness in your life is ok.
- Have confidence to acknowledge the success of others
- Have capacity to forgive and forget
- Feel like you are equipped to handle difficult situations

Column B:

For the most part you:

- Awaken most days lacking optimism or energy
- Worry about how you look
- concerned with how others perceive you
- Are not making or keeping many friends
- Feel worried and sense of dread
- Are isolated from many people
- Wanting to give back and to help other people but unable
- Spend time living in the past and wishing things were different
- Feel resentment for the success of others

- Worry that you are not equipped to deal with difficult people or situations

What if there was a "pill" we could take that would ensure that we lived in Column A, would we take it? What if, instead of a pill, it came in a series of shots, similar to the ones we took for Covid 19 and this would make everyone in society live in column A? What if this particular shot could cure the "depravities" of the human mind that Cicero and Dr. Haidt have been telling us for 2000 years. That, instead of succumbing to our weakest moments, which cause us to close our eyes, and blame others, it would make us keep our eyes open, to actualize our God-given gifts, to move beyond ordinary, to our more natural state of extraordinary? What if this series of immunization shots put an end to bickering politicians forever? We would all line up to take the biggest needle they had- right? Well, what if I told you that such a thing exists and that it doesn't even require a needle. Would we take it? Of course, we would. Let me tell you more about this "pill," because there is a story behind it, and future peace in our society depends on your understanding of this.

I've long had a fascination with the inner workings of the human mind, precisely because of how hard it's been for me to control my own. When I was younger I suffered from anxiety that I never told anyone about. I will never forget my first battle with the anxiety monster. I was a first-year student in law school when I was called on by the professor in my "TORTS" class. At that time, I wouldn't know what a Tort was if it hit me over the head. I was a bit overwhelmed by law school and I was nervous entering the first few classes. When I heard my name called, it happened. My heart tightened to the point of hitting the inner wall of my chest, and my mind seemed to slip out of gear. I began to sweat and the room went dark for a few moments... I couldn't speak. My mind had caused my body to malfunction. Fortunately, the gal next to me, Julie, shoved some notes under my nose and began to talk for me, but I had lost my composure completely. I was totally *dumbfounded*[181] by the experience. The immediate embarrassment of the moment would eventually wear off with time but the experience as a whole has never left me. In fact, to a degree, I believe it shaped how I would live the rest of

---

181. dumbfounded: greatly astonished or amazed

my life. I've had more anxiety attacks since then. I'm pretty sure that it was due to my first experience and my lingering thoughts about it, that guaranteed myself that I would have more.

As they came and went, my shock and awe of them only increased because I thought that I was ready for them- but I never was. I never saw a doctor about them. I had no coaching, no perspective or context for what was happening to me... I just dealt with the anxieties, the fear, and panic, and at some point, something amazing happened- they started to become less severe, even manageable. I sorta self-diagnosed. I told myself that they were simply a part of life and that I would somehow get through them. I chose to think about my mind as this super powerful thing, and that it was my job to learn how to control it. Slowly, instead of being fearful of when the next moment would come, I became almost amused by it and took it as a challenge and I fooled myself into thinking that I was up for the challenge. I decided to flip the script and fight back, no matter how hard it was. But to get to that point took many years.

I was able to get through a few jury trials as a young assistant district attorney I guess by sheer determination. Each time I survived- but barely. It never came easy to me. The night before my first trial I remember not sleeping. I then argued a case in front of the highest court in Massachusetts, the Supreme Judicial Court. I received a letter from the Chief Judge who congratulated me for a job well done, citing my "poise". Imagine that?

Yet, for any success I had at overcoming, the idea that my mind for very little reason could cause my body to become instantly debilitated continued to both bother me and *intrigue*[182] me. Understanding why thoughts would enter my head that I didn't ask for became a fixation of mine. By the time I had children, I began to worry about what I had come to think about as "a situation." I began to wonder if it was possible for me, as a parent, to prepare them and spare them, from "the situation." When I thought they were old enough I gave each of them what I thought to be an age-appropriate pep talk, that went something like this, "hey kiddo, if you feel self doubt, or negative thoughts enter your mind, please understand that they are normal-everyone gets them. You are not alone." That's all I had for them, but I often wondered if that was enough. I was quite confident that I was telling them the truth, but I didn't know for sure. I was just winging it- Sorry kids.

I remember thinking to myself that if I were ever to find the time to research more about "the situation"- this anxiety monster that I was sure was *intrinsic*[183] to the human condition (or to write a book about it?) that I would do so. Then I got wrapped up in my work life and never did. Fast forward a few years, when I found myself without a career. The "going to the library" chapter of my life had finally arrived, and "the situation" was my first area of research. That is why my first chapter is about what scientists tell us about our brains. When I came across Dr. Haidt's teachings about the divided mind and his elephant and rider analogy.. I was *awestruck*[184]. There had never been an intellectual thought that resonated with me more. It was like he had written about my own brain.

Since that moment, I've read just about every book there is about what Dr. Haidt and his colleagues call the new field of "positive psychology." It's an area of study which is as groundbreaking as any new field of knowledge that there has ever been. It has more potential to help the human race than more celebrated technologies such as those that allow Google and Apple to give us Siri and Alexa or the modern engineering that allows us to build skyscrapers to the clouds. It's far more important than those things because it deals with matters of human behavior and

---

182. intrigue: the idea that the senses provide us with direct awareness of objects as they really are.[

183. intrinsic: belonging naturally; essential

184. awestruck: filled with or revealing awe

issues of right versus wrong. All of its concepts are beyond my ability to summarize, but suffice to say that we are talking about an area of diagnoses and treatment that can *immunize*[185] a whole society against the type of ignorance which has held us back for centuries and eventually would give us a *herd mentality*[186] for tolerance. It has not become widely accepted, or adopted, for reasons that I am hoping that you will glean from this book, but the fact that it exists is among the most encouraging things I could ever write to you. It will be the thing that ushers in a whole new era of peace for America, and eventually the world. Here's why:

The ability to engage with other citizens with whom we wildly disagree requires a certain "disposition," and set of skills that are not easily maintained. The harm we are doing to one another comes from our failure to understand or control the faults in ourselves. Without being able to control our natural tendencies-(what I've also referred to as self-mastering) we've struggled. People cannot possibly contribute to cosmopolitanism unless they are able to maintain high virtue in themselves first. The new field of positive psychology deals with all of this- it improves our readiness. It also provides, for the first time ever, practical techniques to reduce our negative thoughts and control our natural anxieties.

As I said, I've been reading for several years now about how to calm my divided mind -and practicing most of the techniques. I'm still terrible at it. I suffer from insomnia which I view as a form of anxiety and I have a very hard time quieting the inner critic in me, whose expectations I am never able to meet. But why do I tell you of my own failure?I figure that I've been working so hard to deal with my divided mind for so many years and I'm still terrible at it, how is it possible that young people - who know nothing about "the situation" could possibly deal with it? We only need to read about all of the unhappiness, suicides, murders, and everyone yelling at each other and hating each other to understand the root cause of all of our problems. People have long suspected that it's the complexities of the human mind

---

185. immunize: make (a person or animal) resistant to a particular infectious disease or pathogen, typically by vaccination.
186. herd mentality: the tendency for people's behavior or beliefs to conform to those of the group to which they belong

that causes all of our problems. So why have we failed to address this?

David Shur, a comedian and television writer wrote a book about his journey to make sense of our crazy world and he said, "The smartest people who have ever lived have been working really hard for thousands of years to try to explain to us how we can be better people, and how we can improve ourselves, but they write so complicatedly and densely and opaquely that no one wants to engage in it... It's like a chef had come up with a recipe for chocolate chip cookies that were both delicious and helped you lose weight, but the recipe was 600 pages long and written in German, and no one read it." (David Shur, Find Page and Book from Prior LTM). Mr. Shur has a point. We also seem to spend a lot of our time giving advice and trying to teach basic life skills to adults who are fully cooked. It seems like a waste of time.

Secondly, the fact is that we never knew what we know today. Just as we invented contact lenses and Lasik Surgery to restore our sight. Scientists have just recently, in the last few years, unlocked the diagnosis and treatment with regard to our loss of regulated thinking. We see more clearly with corrective lenses. It's no different than the corrections we can make to our brains. We know how to treat and cure anxiety and depression better than we have in the past, but far more importantly we have learned how to prevent these conditions. For the first time ever, the same doctors who have diagnosed what causes excessive pride, anxiety, fear, jealousy, vengefulness, depression, and suicidal thoughts, can also prescribe us treatments that prevent these conditions and move us from negative to positive thinkers.

So I need to ask you- What would happen if we were to recognize our new normal as a virus no different than COVID-19? What if we adopted the perspective that one Mass Murder per day is curable, like Covid 19? When people recognized Polio[187], or The Bubonic Plague[188], and Covid[189] as health

---

187. Polio: an infectious disease especially of young children that is caused by the poliovirus
188. The Bubonic Plague: plague caused by a bacterium (Yersinia pestis) and characterized especially by the formation of buboes; Called the Black Death, it killed millions of Europeans during the Middle Ages
189. Covid: Coronavirus disease (COVID-19) is an infectious disease

pandemics capable of wiping out the entire human race, most everyone agreed to get immunized against the disease. Do we not think that our bickering politicians, a country divided, one mass murder every day (list as many bad things you believe are happening in our society here) are as serious a problem?

I believe that our fear, and blaming and demonizing of each other has killed more people than Covid 19, Polio, and the Bubonic Plague combined. If we were to do the math on deaths relating to government failures and *insurrections*[190], and people hating each other- it wouldn't even be close. The problems we are faced with are more dangerous and deadly than any other type of physical virus because it is a virus of the mind. What we have finally come to know as scientific fact is that our minds deceive us. We have never been "smart enough" to fully understand what Cicero meant. Today, we do.

Ryan. A. Bush, is a remarkable young mind, in 2020 summarized some of the world's leading work in the field of positive technology. His book, Designing the Mind (DTM), Bush writes, "The human condition as you know it -is optional. That it is possible for you to unplug from your own mind, examine it from above, and modify the very psychological code on which you operate, permanently altering these limiting patterns" that we find ourselves in. "The mind can be compared to software, made up of many interwoven algorithms which were originally programmed by natural selection. Though most never learn to alter their default programming, it is possible to rewire cognitive biases, change ingrained habits, and transform emotional reactions… DTM is focused on providing wisdom education and expanding human potential beyond the norm. It draws heavily from cognitive therapy, evolutionary psychology, and ancient philosophy…You will learn to build unshakable peace and levity into your mind so you can embrace whatever life throws at you…You will develop the skills to… overcome your own distortions of judgment and cultivate wisdom so you can make the right decisions in your life. You will learn to build the habits, lifestyle, and character which will gradually enable you to become your ideal self." (Bush, 2021)

---

caused by the SARS-CoV-2 virus
190. insurrection: a violent uprising against an authority or government.

Doctor Aaron Beck was the first to coin the term cognitive behavioral therapy or CBT for short. Dr. Haidt writes, "Beck, mapped out the distorted thought processes characteristics of depressed people and trained his patients to catch and challenge these thoughts he created cognitive therapy and one of the most effective treatments available for depression and anxiety and many other problems training clients to catch their thoughts write them down, name the distortions, and then find alternative ways of thinking. Cognitive therapy works because it teaches the rider how to defeat it directly in an argument. On the first day of therapy, the client doesn't realize that the elephant is controlling him, driving his conscious thoughts. Over time, the client learns to use a set of tools; these include challenging automatic thoughts and engaging in simple tasks, such as going out to buy a newspaper rather than staying in bed. Talk therapy teaches us how to distance ourselves from our first automatic impulse, step away from it, measure it, feel for how ordinary it is, and then move beyond it. (Haidt, 2006, p. 35)

Dr. Haidt says, "You can't win a tug of war with an angry elephant, but you can -by gradually shaping the sort of behaviorist talk about- change your automatic thoughts and in the process your affective style. Life is what we deem it, and our lives are the creations of our minds, but these claims are not helpful until augmented by a theory of the divided self (such as the rider and the elephant) and understanding of negativity bias and affective style. Once you know why change is so hard, **you can drop the brute force method and take a more psychologically sophisticated approach to self-improvement... you need a method for taming the elephant, for changing your mind gradually...through awareness of the modern science of how the brain operates, and treatment redeem yourself."** (Haidt, 2006, p. 37) Training ourselves to think, with our rider in control is possible. **"by drawing on humanity's greatest ideas and best science, we can train the elephant, know our possibilities as well as our limits, and can live wisely"**(Haidt, 2006, p. 243).

So congratulations. I know this may seem a little premature. But your generation is the first to have a cure for what has ailed us for centuries. The process by which we build up distrust of one another is one that is preventable. Like an auto mechanic can free up the gunk that builds up in an engine, or like a computer programmer reprograms a computer, modern-day researchers can teach us how to improve the way we process information and become less fearful of one another. We can all grow up to be more self-confident, and to defer our most harmful first impulses. We can lower the amount of jealousy we have for other people. We can learn how to be better at affirming the good in others. We can limit our instincts to wanna always be right, and to take the credit. We can learn how to feel more confident to join community discussions about difficult topics and equip ourselves to do the difficult work of citizenship. Given a little time, we can and will develop a herd immunity to the type of ordinary, resentful, angry, or sleepwalking modes and mindsets that have been holding us back. In time, extreme news outlets and misinformation stations will disappear as people become more aware of their own bias and we stop tuning into those channels that play on our preconceived prejudices.

Acceptance is the first step in any form of recovery. All one future generation of young Americans needs to do is accept the problems we have in our society as a national health crisis, and you will solve the puzzle. It is our obligation as a human race to help people avoid degenerating and to prepare people to be good citizens. With a little urging, your generation will be the first to gain collective commitment to focus on education that keeps everyone upright and strong, rather than flimsy and weak. It was Martin Luther King who said, "We must learn together as brothers or perish together as Fools."

The largest weapon we have to improve the world is empathy. As you develop your empathy, and other skills which build your emotional resiliency you begin to ensure your own well-being. Today we know to a scientific degree of certainty how we hold onto the good stuff, rather than let the bad stuff get to us. The more you understand the secrets which strengthen your brain, you can take yourself to higher levels of personal satisfaction and success. At the highest levels, you become a leader, capable of re-igniting the internal flame of goodness that resides in others, particularly those who need it most.

As more of you gain these skills, the part of the human brain we need will become stronger over time, and eventually, our whole species will evolve for the better. It will become more typical for your kids, my grandkids, and their children to be born internally wired to handle the demands of society. Politics and life for everyone will become easier when everyone is educated- This is our Breakthrough.

Chapter 11: Deadly Myths

We've never chosen to deal with our never-ending societal problems for what they are; One large mental health crisis, where hurt people, hurt people. Instead, our government priorities and policies have been determined in large part by a bunch of myths built on fear. This is why we are living in such abnormal and divided times. What we are seeing is that between greatly imagined enemies anything goes and words themselves become weapons of good vs. evil. Words that used to be the bedrock of our society, and for which we have relied on for centuries to hold us together, such as knowledge, diversity, equity, and inclusion, have become sources of deep division. Words like Defund the Police, White Privilege, Indoctrination, Censorship, all become like *dog whistles*[191] with attached meanings. In our war of extremes these words have become *casualties*[192] People have basically scared the shit out of one another.

Before the breakthrough, I introduced the concept of myths. Myths are those things that develop like a rainbow at the end of a perfect storm, except instead of being full of light and color, they represent our darkness. Myths invade people like *pestilence*[193] that creeps along the ground, and up our legs, and slowly into our hearts and minds. To be clear, if there is evil in this world, the myths we allow to exist in our society are the greatest evil we face. Myths are the mechanism by which the few tear down the many. We wouldn't have haters if we didn't have myths. With each mass shooting, it is the myths that we allow to *infiltrate*[194] in our society that are behind the excuses we make, which *sanction* more acts of hate. When well intentioned Americans,

---

191. dog whistle: a subtly aimed political message which is intended for, and can only be understood by, a particular group
192. casualties: a person killed or injured in a war or accident.
193. pestilence: a fatal epidemic disease, especially bubonic plague
194. infiltrate: enter or gain access to (an organization, place, etc.) surreptitiously and gradually, especially in order to acquire secret information

whom we should rightfully *emulate*[195] are *slandered*[196], insulted, and even assassinated- it is the same myths that give safe haven to those who provide justification, that *rationalize*[197] the offenders' behaviors, and slowly but surely reduce our collective outrage, rendering our response futile.

Our 38th President of the United States, and great philosopher, John Fitzgerald Kennedy, (JFK) identified the dangers of made-up myths in a commencement speech, June 11, 1962, to a graduating class at the aforementioned Yale University, in New Haven CT. He said, "The great enemy of truth is very often not the lie – deliberate, contrived and dishonest–but the myth– persistent, persuasive and unrealistic. Too often we hold fast to the cliches of our forebears. We subject all facts to a prefabricated set of interpretations. **We enjoy the comfort of opinion, without the discomfort of thought.**" The "comfort of opinion without the discomfort of thought." What do you think JFK meant by this? By not thinking deeply enough we create false realities. He warned us that playing casual with facts is deadly.

As promised, I want to look at a few of these myths in detail, starting with the deadliest of all: The "myth of education." The myth that universal education is a danger, rather than the foremost thing that is capable of producing our model society, is the most destructive of all the myths we are currently faced with.

Today's favorite word used by our all too ordinary politicians is- "Indoctrination." The word itself, minus any added meaning, simply means " to teach or instruct" but today it is used by those stuck in second gear as a fear tactic. Is there anything so bad or negative about being indoctrinated as a deep thinker? Is it bad for us to be taught to believe that there is a flame of goodness in all human beings, or to instead of first suspecting a person, to affirm the good in them? Is it bad to teach the importance of having a growth mindset, that is, that we can change our outlook

---

195. emulate: match or surpass (a person or achievement), typically by imitation.
196. slander: make false and damaging statements about (someone)
197. rationalize: attempt to explain or justify (one's own or another's behavior or attitude) with logical, plausible reasons, even if these are not true or appropriate

by merely changing our attitude? Is it bad to try to indoctrinate into all young Americans the idea that to pursue wisdom and knowledge is to pursue happiness? Of course not- in fact our being widely indoctrinated with these beliefs is our only chance of improving things.

However today a request from one person to another, to be more sensitive about how we communicate, or to be more tolerant of someone or something, comes across as an illegitimate attempt by one person to brainwash another. Nowadays, if anyone talks about the importance of greater understanding- of anything- They are suspected as being part of some socialistic woke mob. In our new normal, it's become UnAmerican to be awake or woke. Today, if someone mentions that they went to college at Harvard (Est. 1636), or Princeton (Est. 1746) or Yale (Est. 1701), they are looked down upon. They are thought about as being out-of-touch *elitists*[198]. The great problem with all this is that our society is in *shambles*[199]. If we are going to share society we need to share standards of behavior. The only way to create shared standards of behavior is to teach and educate the same thing. And I'm not talking about learning the ABC's or basic math. I am only talking about education concerning natural law, and what it means to be a good citizen. We need a mandatory common curriculum of these things.Remember, there is no bogeyman behind some curtain that is responsible for our destiny. It is just us. When we lose faith in government, we lose faith in our government run schools. Loss of faith in our public schools, as of late, has caused a disastrous outcome.

Just a few years ago the belief that a formal system of education, which would teach the responsibilities of citizenship, was the foundational building block behind everything. This is supported in thousands of quotations from the people who were involved in forming our system of government. "The English colonists in America undertook something which no nation had ever attempted before- the educating of the whole people. The colonists had a sense of "manifest destiny" which led them to believe that they must prepare themselves for a most unique and all-important role in the unfolding of modern world history.

---

198. elitist: a person who believes that a society or system should be led by an elite
199. shambles: a state of total disorder

Universal education was therefore considered an indispensable ingredient in this preparation." (Haidt, 2006, p. 249)It was a widely accepted fact that "a free society cannot survive as a republic without a broad program of general education." Thomas Jefferson said, "Liberty cannot be preserved without a general knowledge among the people"(Skousen, 1981, p. 50) "Bigotry is the disease of ignorance, of morbid minds ... education & free discussion are the antidotes of both." (August 1, 1816, Library of Congress). Jefferson also said- "I've often thought that nothing would do more extensive good at small expense than the establishment of a small circulating library in every county, to consist of a few well-chosen books, to be lent to the people of the country under regulations that would secure their safe return in due time." (Thomas Jefferson to John Wyche, May 19, 1809, The Library of Congress).

Of the Americans, visiting French Philosopher Alexis Detoqueville observed, "In New England, every citizen receives the elementary notions of human knowledge; he is taught moreover, the doctrines and the evidence of his religion, the history of his country, and the leading features of its Constitution. In the states of Connecticut and Massachusetts, it is extremely rare to find a man imperfectly acquainted with all these things, and a person wholly ignorant of them is a sort of phenomenon. "(Skousen, 1981, pp. 250–252) quote "Education of all ranks of people was made at the care and expense of the public, in a manner that I believe has been unknown to any other people, ancient or modern. The consequences of these establishments we see and feel every day. A native of America who cannot read or write is as rare... as a comet or an earthquake. It has been observed that we are all of us lawyers, divines, politicians, and philosophers. <u>And I have good authority to say that all candid foreigners who have passed through this country and conversed freely with all sorts of people here will allow that they have never seen so much knowledge and civility among the common people in any part of the world...</u>"

"One of the most amazing aspects of the American story is that while the nation's founders came from widely divergent backgrounds, their fundamental beliefs were virtually identical... They came from different churches, and some from no churches at all. They ranged in occupations from farmers to presidents of universities. Their dialects included everything from southern drawls, from poverty to wealth. How is one to possibly explain their remarkable unanimity in fundamental beliefs? "While the nation's founders came from widely divergent backgrounds, they were able to learn how to communicate, and to keep things ordered and peaceful... Perhaps the explanation will be found in the fact that they were all remarkably well read..." "Although the level of their formal training varied... the debates in the Constitutional Convention and the writings of the Founders reflect a far broader knowledge of religious, political, historical, economic and philosophical studies than would be found in a cross-section of American leaders today... To this writer, nothing is more remarkable about the early American leaders than their breadth of reading and depth of knowledge concerning the essential elements of sound nation-building." (Skousen, 1981, pp. 31–32)

The last hurdle in any race is the tallest one. To get adults to accept there may be something lacking in us, and that our own ignorance is responsible for holding our society back- has proven to be very hard. If I could snap my fingers and make everyone accept that ignorance, even of the unintentional kind, is our problem, that would mean that we would all accept that universal education is key to our success. We would adapt and change our government policies to focus on early education in all our schools of natural law, of kindness, acceptance, and citizenship training. We would focus on providing every American a well-rounded "liberal arts" education, as opposed to a single trade education. We would modify our trade schools and make our affordable community colleges more well-rounded so that young people receive the type of education that ensures that they would never get stuck in second gear. But that is not us today. Today we are setting policies in response to our myths -not our reality. We are draining public schools of resources and directing taxpayer money toward private school vouchers. These policies will guarantee that we further segregate along race, color, and class differences.

There is no doubt all who receive a college-level education are lucky people. There is no doubt that this particular type of education gives people fulfillment and happiness, and in many cases fame and money. We need to make every American that lucky. If we don't, the misfortune of the uneducated will continue to represent and define the misfortune of all of us. Education is our only hope, it always was, and always will be. Ignorance leads to chaos and political disagreement. "The multitude of the wise is the welfare of the world."(Book of Solomon 6:24, Apocrypha). When will we learn?

The next myth I want to talk about is the one that has people believing that all government is bad and can't fix anything. I know I hit on this earlier, but now I want to close the loop. In reality, the government is good, and can and does fix things every day. We in fact have thousands upon thousands of great politicians, who you could trust with your most prized possessions. But that is not what the myth says. We are doing a lousy job of teaching kids about all the good the government does. I'm not for big government, but we need some government. The fact is that we need to gain control over something that is wildly out of control. Right now our government isn't working. Do we need to limit regulation?- Yes, as much as we can. Do we need to balance a budget? Yes. (A government should use debt wisely, and always have the ability to pay back its debts). Should we limit taxes as much as possible? Yes. Should we let people be as free as they can possibly be? Yes. But we are NOT free to stop relying on organized government to educate each other. Our failure to place our priority on universal values education has been our downfall. I believe I've established what the few things are that I would prioritize teaching to young people in high school, but if I've not been clear, the follow-up work on my website aims to make the curriculum clear, and concise. There are three books on my website that I believe most accurately set forth the mechanisms of national government as the founders intended it to be, and therefore should be among those books which are the basis for a core universal civics education. I am in the process of trying to get the authors to make the content more accessible for young people- and into the schools in a more digestible fashion. Until then- Please try as you can to read them.* Also, we need to do a

*https://gettingalong.com/resources/5000-year-leap
https://gettingalong.com/resources/if-you-can-keep-it
https://gettingalong.com/resources/the-american-presidency

much better job of circulating facts about all the good that the government does. I will be making an effort to do this on the site, but we need the effort to be more widely adopted to *debunk*[200] the myth that the government is bad.

---

200. debunk: expose the falseness or hollowness of (a <u>myth</u>, idea, or belief)

It's just not true. The word *Censorship*[201] is the last example of a word that is today being misused by *uninspired*[202] politicians causing America deep heartache and stress when its real meaning is as simple as the word love or kindness. Our understanding of its true meaning would cause the world to come together, and unite. Every organized society needs some control over things that people say. In reality, it's not anti-American to censor stupid shit. It's anti-American to keep saying stupid shit. But instead, we can no longer agree on what stupidity looks like. The myth of censorship and the related issues of free speech are so important I will try to tackle them in the next chapter.

I want to switch now to another big myth that may be less talked about. It's the myth that "Money Can't Buy You Happiness". This is a cultural myth that has been used for years to justify great disparities in income. Some people say it to make themselves feel better, and that is understandable. Taken alone the myth may not seem that harmful. In fact, I'm sure it's true for some individuals- That money doesn't buy happiness, but as a societal lie the subtle nature of this myth makes it one of our most dangerous.

If we are being honest, anyone who has flown first class, or gotten a three-hour massage on a beach while sipping a pina colada (which I believe Sally and Bob equally enjoy) would tell you that money can and absolutely does buy happiness. That is precisely why people with money work so hard (and act like such assholes) to keep it, and it is why people without money want more of it. On this point, can you blame any person or family who has lived for generations in poverty for wanting a little bit more of what other people have? In the alternative, can we really blame those people who have lived in comfort and with financial wealth to want to hold on to what they have ? Of course not. The reason for this is clear, for the most part, if we are seeing through the myth- money does buy happiness.

Instead of creating some cross-understanding and mutual respect for each other. I'd like to see your generation grow up to be a

---

201. censorship: the suppression or prohibition of any parts of books, films, news, etc. that are considered obscene, politically unacceptable, or a threat to security.
202. uninspired: lacking in imagination or originality.

little more straightforward and honest with one another- to bridge the economic classes. It's another myth that people casually go along with that creates great distance between the haves and have-nots.

The "money doesn't buy you happiness" myth leads into a more damaging myth. This is the one that says that people living in poverty can live happy lives. This is mostly bullshit. If they do manage to break out of poverty and lead mostly happy lives, they should be given a lot more credit than they are being given. David Goggins, one of my mentors, grew up in poverty. About it he writes, "When kids like me grow up, they face increased risk for clinical depression, heart disease, obesity, and cancer, not to mention smoking, alcoholism and drug abuse... those raised in abusive household have an increased probability of being arrested as a juvenile by 53%, their odds of committing a violent crime as an adult are increased by 38%... toxic stress... leads to learning disabilities and social anxiety because according to doctors it limits language development and memory, which makes it difficult for even the most gifted student to recall what they have already learned... (Goggins, 2021, p. 41). People who grow up without support systems or enough money to have necessities, they do not live happy lives. For us to think any different is the most cowardly, and un-American myth of them all. And we should all be ashamed. Our big cities today are littered with the disease which is poverty. And as the rest of us visit cities like New Orleans and Manhattan or downtown San Francisco or Detroit, and walk around those suffering from mental health problems due to growing up in poverty, and without the type of education spoken about in Myth 1, we should be embarrassed- we've let these people suffer such indignities. We've allowed our urban centers to decay into examples of human tragedy... all as a result of our not paying enough attention to what is truly expected of us, in this life.

But because of lies, and myths, that we tell ourselves it has become American to expect people to overcome such toxic inputs in their lives when it is not possible. **The people who are living in wealthy communities enjoy the comfort of their own opinion, without the discomfort of real thought. Or they conveniently choose to believe that it's someone else's problem to fix. Well, it's not. It's all our problem to fix. We are all in this mess together (NL 102).** We are all smart enough to know that people living on the streets in the inner city, waiting in bread lines, or on *welfare*[203] didn't wake up one day and decide, I want to be poor. They may have made some bad choices, and maybe they don't deserve to be driving a Mercedes and eating prime cut filet mignon every night like someone who worked very hard and earned the money- but most of us know how to balance these considerations. We are smart enough to know (NL 101) that NO human being should live in a state of destitute poverty.

The last myth I need to discuss may be the hardest one for anyone to accept- particularly if you are a man. To be a rugged tough guy and masculine individualist, in our country is a brand unto itself. There is only one little problem- In <u>reality</u>, our form of government doesn't do well under what we currently celebrate as a male-dominated value system. In his book "If You Can Keep It- The Forgotten Promise of American Liberty," Eric Metaxas writes: "The experiment in liberty called America is not something easily or intuitively grasped." "The government they had given us was something precious and fragile, a newborn babe for whom all of us were obliged to care."(Metaxas, 2016, p. 18) When we read what the people who wrote our Constitution and who fought and died for our country really thought about what American freedom stands for, it becomes crystal clear that the only muscle that our founding fathers used in creating our government was their brain. The success of our country's government systems had nothing to do with *brawn*[204]. Our government is not designed to be ruled with an iron-handed approach, but yet our myths give us a seemingly endless appetite for heavy doses of testosterone in our leaders.The plain truth is that masculine guys suck as leaders. Masculine pride and masculine ignorance has ruined our government, but of course, it is not popular to speak this truth. Women are not our problem. Men have always been our problem. I say this will all due respect to women everywhere.

Now, before you chalk me up as a liberal sally- please remember, this is coming from the guy who rented the midget for a ninety-man bachelor party in Vegas! In fact, at this moment

---

203. welfare: financial support given to people in need.
204. brawn: physical strength in contrast to intelligence

I am so desperate for you to take my advice as *credible*[205] and in order to save my masculinity, I've chosen this moment to blow my cover. I've been a registered Republican my whole life, more of a Bob than a Sally. But here is the deal. I'd like to think that I am a- "Thinking Bob." I want my daughter to marry a thinking Bob. Masculinity is great, as long as it comes with the ability to think like JFK or MLK. To our non-thinking Bobs- Drop your manly bullshit, drop your pride. Be a real man- which is a thinking man. Be kind and compassionate- to everyone, no matter their race, religion, etc. Your masculinity isn't as cool as you think. Your intolerance is ugly. As kids who are reading this book and others continue to learn and grow all around you... You are becoming a dinosaur. You are losing at the game of life. Your toughness is working against you- it's creating a worse future for your grandkids. When you look in the mirror, your unhappiness will only grow. This isn't a threat, it's only based on all of the advice in the library, a place that you should go. I have no problem putting myself in the Sally category if I can reveal the truth. The truth is found in the books that people write, and in the words that people read. Not in the false myths limited to a Twitter post, or from some kid who is acting like his uneducated tough guy father on the playground. I just hope my wife is still talking to me after she reads this entry.

The thing about myths is that they stack on each other and blend together. They are like streams that converge together to form a mighty river. For example, our recently exaggerated fear of the word Censorship is very much related to the myth of endless American Freedom. The fear of the word Indoctrination is linked to the fear of big government and the deep blue state. Our fascist politicians jumble all of the big myths together. The *strategic*[206] and *tactical*[207] compiling of myths is what makes them so dangerous. Like a doctor uses a scalpel, fascist politicians use the *commingling*[208] of myths to gain a microphone and keep a platform that they otherwise would not have. They use generalizations and talk loosely about facts in order to keep the

---

205. credible: able to be believed; convincing.
206. strategic: relating to the identification of long-term or overall aims and interests and the means of achieving them
207. tactical: relating to or constituting actions carefully planned to gain a specific military end
208. commingle: mix, blend

myths in the forefront and keep people in fear of each other. They create a "they" vs "us" society. They are selling us false goods. They are playing on our fears, and perpetuating false myths. Their fear tactics ensure that we fight a raging fire with more fire. When in real life, fire is fought with water.

Earlier in the book I made a promise to you that I would not blame Mr. Donald Trump, our 45th President, for anything that I didn't blame myself for. However, while writing this book, I had hoped that things in America would improve. I was actually hoping for Mr. Trump and the people who had supported him in the past could awaken to see the errors he is making. Sadly, that hasn't occurred, in fact, I've become more afraid for our country than when I first sat down to write my birthday card to my son. I read in the paper recently, Mr. Trump saying to a group of his supporters, "sinister forces trying to kill America seek to create a socialist dumping ground for criminals, junkies, Marxists, thugs, radicals, and dangerous refugees" and that "If those opposing us succeed, our once beautiful USA will be a failed country that no one will recognize. A lawless, open borders, crime-ridden, filthy, communist nightmare." (Fins, 2023) None of this is true. These are great exaggerations which are tearing our country apart. A leader's job is to cool our passions, not inflame them, but yet that is what Mr. Trump and other fascist politicians do. All they do is call attention to our differences, rather than to point out our similarities. They spread lies of rigged elections and call into question our voting systems when there is no factual proof of any errors. They call into question the integrity of our legal system and cause us to question the goodness of our longstanding schools. They place blame on everyone but themselves. They never take the time to look in the mirror or work hard to explain to the other side that they hear them, and respect them, even if they disagree with them. They offer no solutions to complex problems. They are like broken records, with no original thoughts. These types of politicians are having a crushing effect on millions of people. For some reason, I remain hopeful that Mr. Trump, who is running for President in 2024, will come to awaken and see the error in his ways. I am also hopeful that the fascist politicians on the other side of the political spectrum will wake up to their mistakes.

It's been 60 years since JFK asked us to be a society of deep thinkers and tried to remind us that casual thought is insufficient for the work of citizenship- particularly for those who run for higher office. Today, the carelessness of our new breed of non-philosopher, fascist politician, seems to know no bounds and society's tolerance for the chaos which their carelessness creates is at an all-time high. A little over a year after giving us this warning, JFK was shot and killed... by a hater. (Nov 2, 1963). MLK, another great philosopher who worked with JFK on peacemaking, was assassinated on April 4, 1968, by another hater.

JFK and MLK believed in natural law. They knew that closed-mindedness leads to the downplaying of the importance of education, which leads to a distorted view of reality and a society with no collective identity. They knew that individual acts of hate are a reflection of our whole society. We did not heed their words, and we lost two of the greatest people that ever lived. The truth is that their blood is on every adult's hand. It will be on your hands soon. The adult generation has failed to summon the courage to stop the lies and the spinning of our deadly myths. Will your generation allow our myths to control our society?

The truth is not always always easy to see, and it's even harder to speak. In large numbers, we are often not as courageous as we need to be. Some people believe that only God gives us the superpowers to find the courage to protect the truth from the forces that fight against it. Harold Kushner, in his book, Living a Life That Matters, writes "If the words you speak are hard for you to utter and hard for others to hear, if you get no pleasure from speaking them but you feel you must, then you can believe that they come from God." (Kushner, 2011, p. 95) It could be that this is what it feels like to be operating in the mode JFK asked us to. It is a mode of thinking where you are reaching deep to find the right conclusion- one that might not serve your personal interests, but one that is most consistent with reason, and therefore is most consistent with nature.

In his best-selling book, "The Good Life" Peter J. Gomes, a minister at Harvard College for more than 30 years, (1942-2011) "distinguishes between the **plausible lies** that our culture tells us about the good life and the fantastic truths that alone can bring true and abiding happiness." (Gomes, 2009, pt. Intro) "Perhaps it will help us to know that such virtues exist, can be taught and learned, and must be practiced... what follows is an effort to discuss these virtues, these fantastic truths, **against the backdrop of the *plausible* lies that are meant to '*confute*[209]'**... The good life is the one that is lived in pursuit of those fantastic truths that endure in times such as these. "(Gomes, 2009, pt. 48) Similarly, in his book Morality, Sir Jonathan Sacks writes "When we move from the politics of "Me" to the politics of "Us," we rediscover those life-transforming, *counterintuitive truths:* that a nation is strong when it cares for the weak, that it becomes rich when it cares for the poor, that it becomes invulnerable when it cares for the vulnerable... There is no liberty without morality, no freedom without responsibility, no viable 'I' without the sustaining 'We'."(Sacks, 2020, p. 20)

I cannot stress enough the importance of your recognizing these counterintuitive truths as the basis for positive change in our complex society. I know one thing for sure, our frontal lobes need to prevail. In fact, to be "woke" is our only chance of avoiding the extinction of the whole human race. How is that for a counterintuitive truth? There are adults who are lying to you. They don't mean to, but they are. You can either take that advice or leave it, but in time, just do me a favor if you don't see the world around you becoming a better place to be, just keep this chapter- about myths- in mind.

---

209. confute: prove (a person or an assertion) to be wrong.

Chapter 12: Voices of Evil and Types of Harm

I have to say something about evil. I admit that it exists. However, as you might recall from chapter one, I don't think it's born into people. Rather, I believe, people experience the input of toxins or traumatic conditions after birth which attach to their hearts and grow worse without treatment. This causes some to become evil and to carry out horrific acts of violence that only people of pure evil could. I certainly don't know if God plants evil into some people prior to birth and inserts them into our world just to make things that much more interesting down here- knowing something like this is well above my pay grade. Plus, on this subject, it doesn't matter what I think. The powers that control things down here seem to want humankind to have to deal with the worst of the worst, and we will. In this book, I don't want to focus on what I am calling pure evil, those who commit unspeakable acts of violence like rape and murder. I choose to leave issues of crime and punishment for that type of evil to your generation to figure out, and as said- you will. What I would like to talk about is a totally different type of evil. That is the voice of evil. I believe that voices of evil are doing a lot more damage to our society than those who are committing acts of violence, and stopping them is proving to be much harder than stopping our violent criminals. I say this with great respect for victims of violent crimes everywhere. Please let me explain.

We have a very strong legal system in place to deal with violent crimes. We are actually quite good at it. As football coach Bill Belichek might say, we "play well in all phases of the game." From investigating to prosecuting and convicting, our violent criminals most often get caught and are locked up or committed to death. We most often get our revenge on violent criminals. Punishing them is also a source of great pride for our local communities, and for our nation as well. From local police to state police to the FBI (Federal Bureau of Investigation) to the Department of Justice, various groups of law enforcement come together to fight those who pose a threat to our physical well-being. Pure evil is a common enemy, and there is no stronger bonding agent for Americans than to defeat a common enemy.

The sense of *patriotism*[210] felt after we captured and killed *Osama Bin Laden*[211], or when we caught and killed the sick brothers who bombed us in Boston on *Patriots Day*[212] 2013 are good examples of this.

However, when it comes to voices of evil, we have nothing going on. We don't have a coach, we don't have a team. In fact, we do not even play the game. Instead of having a system which could be a source of American pride, to tame the voices which are pulling us down and tearing us apart, we have the opposite-we have a **national disaster** on our hands.

I often see this guy at the golf driving range I go to. His name is Bob. I swear, I cannot make this stuff up... Bob is sorta fat. Sorry, I am SO bad... I hope my book has been balanced enough for me to say a few things like this. The club has a rule about tucking in your shirt. Bob's shirt is always hanging out and not only that, it always has some spaghetti sauce somewhere on it, typically below the chin area. Bob is always sweating in all the wrong places but other than that, Bob seems extremely comfortable with himself. He's usually smoking a fat cigar, which apparently enhances his level of comfort and relaxation. His voice is loud which makes the fact that he's always striking up conversations with people very noticeable. Most often, it's about politics. The other day Bob approached me, "Hey buddy boy" he says, (Bob, calls everyone Buddy Boy... I'm not quite sure why) jumping right in with politics, "Did you see what's going on at the southern border? We are letting every illegal wet-back Mexican and Guatemalan cross the border and come into our country for free! They're all criminals, none of them speak our language, and we are taking care of them! They are taking our jobs, filling our schools, and selling drugs to our kids. We gotta get this current stupid asshole out of the Oval Office or our whole country is gonna look like Haiti!" ...

---

210. patriotism: the quality of being patriotic; devotion to and vigorous support for one's country

211. Osama bin Laden: also known as Usama bin Laden—was a violent terrorist and mass murderer who used bombings and bloodshed to advance his extremist goals

212. Patriots' Day: the anniversary of the battles of Lexington and Concord (1775), celebrated the third Monday in April: a legal holiday in Massachusetts and Maine

Hmmmmmmmm- I thought to myself… I've got a class A, non-thinking Bobby on my hands, a real live bucking bronco in the flesh. This guy would make my Uncle Donny look like my Aunt Sally. What should I do? First, diffuse the situation, I'm thinking to myself, cool his passion, and don't poke the bear in the wild… My mind raced with an appropriate response… I stuttered awkwardly and said, "That is certainly one way of looking at things, Bob." That is all I could come up with. Then I quickly turned and excused myself, as if I had to take a poop or throw up or something… "Sorry, I just need to use the restroom." I said as I bolted away from him, as usual.

How much harm do you think Bob is doing? Do you think he cares? Of course, he doesn't care. However, he doesn't care because he doesn't know any better. Do you think Bob is visiting the JFK Library and Museum on the weekends and learning about myths? Of course, he isn't. But if he doesn't know any better, then how can he be blamed? He really can't be.

So what do we do about Bob? How do we deal with this great complication of not being able to blame people, when we know what they are saying is not helpful, or downright hurtful? We can't just go around calling people stupid. That would only show the type of shortsightedness that got us into our problems in the first place. But at the same time, we need to try to get our arms around how people speak to one another, so we can achieve a better society, one that is based on the natural laws of self-mastery and cosmopolitanism. If we don't do this how are we ever going to put an end to our haters and myths spreaders? We need to call out ignorance for what it is and establish some standards of acceptable and unacceptable behaviors, but how? Can we change Bob? (Can we change our bucking broncos, our haters, and all those who have come detached from the natural laws?) This is the million-dollar question.

First thing is first. It's worth repeating… never approach a bucking bronco in the wild! You are not going to ever get a Bronco to stop bucking while he is in "mid buck"… His elephant brain is busy tossing his rational self, and he is in no mindset to be talked to at that moment. We need to "wait the bronco out" and only address him or her when you are surrounded by other 90%ers. I will complete my ideas shortly as to whether we can change Bob, but first I want to take a closer look at the origins of this great challenge we face because it is obvious that every generation before yours has failed to address our largest problem- our not being able to call out harmful speech for what it is. What makes it so hard?

We all know what moments of moral destruction look like. We've talked about this. Our internal radar for knowing when we are in the presence of someone who is saying or doing something morally incorrect is incredibly strong. However, that doesn't make it any easier to intervene or get involved when those lines are crossed, does it? We witness moments of sheer stupidity all the time, day after day stupid moment after stupid moment. We can actually feel these moments sucking the intended life out of us- because that is what they are doing, they are literally sucking the intended life out of everyone. Yet, none of us know what to do in these situations. It's like watching an impending trainwreck, knowing of the impact, but you can't do anything to stop it.

Physical harm is easy to see, it causes us to bleed. This is why we dedicate billions of dollars a year to defend ourselves against enemies that threaten our physical safety, with an Army and a Navy, Air Force, and Marines. Words cut as deeply as knives do, but the damage is not as visible. Therefore, when people are acting like idiots, saying hateful things, dividing us into two camps, etc., we are caught helpless- like a "deer in headlights." We have no structure, no process, no patience or understanding. We are totally lost. We just accept Bob for who he is. Maybe shake our heads left and right a few times in disbelief, but then go on with our day. We also play it off as though Bob is just having a bad day, that his sheer display of ignorance is a temporary thing. But all too often being an unthinking Bob is a permanent condition. In America, we go along pretending that they aren't a problem when in reality, they are a huge problem. Therefore, **nothing changes, decade after decade.**

What about the law? Shouldn't it help us? Having been lucky to go to law school, I can tell you that our laws concerning our First Amendment (which people commonly refer to as "our right to freedom of speech") are among the most brilliantly written and are totally inspiring. They are built on something called "*case law*" where people like you and me argue their sides to juries, made up of people like you and me, who make the decisions which shape our written laws. Having been created by people like you and me, you might think that we would follow our laws and that our laws would come to represent who we are. Oliver Wendell Homes Jr. Associate Justice United States Supreme Court (1902-1932) was heard to say, "The Law is the witness and external deposit of our moral life. Its history is the history of the moral development of the race." In theory, our laws were intended to be a codified or structured system of shared values. However, in practice, our laws only lurk in the distant background of our day-to-day reality. In a culture dominated by myths, written laws become junk science, not worth the paper they are written on- millions of people assume that the laws were created falsely, and by people who do not serve their interests.

Hardly anybody reads our laws. We don't teach First Amendment law in our public schools. We do not prioritize learning. Add in our natural inclination to feel our way through life rather than think through it, freedom of speech begins to FEEL very similar to our right to wear underwear or not, or to plant tomatoes in your yard. That is why people tend to freak out if anyone tries to come up with any new ideas to regulate or control how people speak to one another. Today if someone (like me) mentions the word censorship, they would have to duck for cover... when in reality, some censorship is <u>exactly</u> what we need to have a civilized society. We don't stand a chance against our myths.

What makes these matters even more challenging, is the fact that it's hard to limit speech in a way that is fair because we don't want to empower some authority like a dictator, authoritarian, or overreaching centralized government to decide what is good speech or bad speech. The development of the human race depends on the unrestricted flow of ideas and thoughts. Ideas that stretch the imagination or even those that shock us at first, provide us context, information, and perspective that we would otherwise lack. Think about it, if we had allowed some authority to quiet the person who first said that the earth was not flat, but rather round, where would we be? So we need to be super careful with how we create laws, which limit the free flow of ideas, or to infringe in any way, on what people want to do while in private. On the other hand, we are smart enough to know that certain ideas, and thoughts spoken in public lead to the type of messed up society we have now. If we were to agree with Justice

Holmes, about the law "being the witness and external deposit of our moral life", then we might agree that the debate over words and associated behaviors that are acceptable or not goes to the very essence of who we are. So who are we? The other day I was listening to the radio and this song came on, and went something like this:

> We the people in all we do
> Reserve the right to scream "Fuck You"
> (Hey -yeah) Ow
> (Hey -yeah) HUH.
> Wear your mask, take your pills'
> Now a whole generation is mentally ill.
> Hey yeah Man, Fuck Fauci.
> But COVIDS near, it's coming to town.
> We gotta act quick, shut our borders down!
> Joe Biden does, the media embraces.
> Big Don does it and they call him a racist.
> We the people (woo, Let's go Brandon)
> We the people (woo, Let's go Brandon)
> We the people (woo, Let's go Brandon)
> We the people. Fuck Facebook
> Fuck Twitter too,
> And the mainstream media, fuck you too, too too
> Woo Yeah You."

We The People, by Kid Rock

Before the song ends I think I can hear him telling me to suck on something... called theezzz... I'm pretty sure he meant his ballsack... (sorry... but I'm trying to make my point here). Also "lets go Brandon" means Fuck Joe Biden... Ahhh, the beauty of the myth of American freedom and free speech- on full display! We FEEL we are the land of the free, yet we never THINK about the fact that we have more people locked up in America than in all of the other major countries in the world combined! (*Incarceration Rates by Country 2023*, n.d.) We FEEL free to tell our President to Fuck off, and everyone else to suck our balls on public radio, and that feels pretty darn good- so maybe it's worth it? We are the best, aren't we?

Yet my friends eat this stuff up. They buy the Let's Go Brandon T-shirts just to be funny, notwithstanding they aren't even into politics, some don't even vote. My own kids do it too. They send *memes* about Joe Biden being old and forgetful like the one where he is hugging the Easter Bunny while saying Merry Christmas. The other day my son John showed me a video from Truth Social (President Trump's social media channel) where Trump hits a golf ball and hits President Biden in the head knocking him over. My liberal friends send me memes about Trump, how he cheats at golf. They call me Sally for not participating in the text strings. This is just the way things are right? I'm sure you and your friends are doing the same things.

Everyone accepts the jokes and strongly believes that they have the right to say and do whatever they want. And they would be correct under our written laws. But does that mean that they should? Or that they have an accurate understanding of the First Amendment? Of course not. Their understanding of our laws only goes as far as our myths allow them to, and they have a very distorted understanding of our laws. **Our behaviors are shaped by our myths, not our laws. This is why nothing changes.**

The media is another voice of evil, worse than our musicians and our friends. All they do is give us the bad news. Let me give you an example. I read the Boston Globe Newspaper on most days. It's always negative. I look for positive stories and when they exist, they are barely findable on the bottom of the page, in small print. Just the other day, I found this really small article, a few sentences long, about how our Federal government spent **$68 Billion dollars** on wireless internet connections for low-income and remote area access.(*Broadband Equity Access and Deployment Program | BroadbandUSA*, n.d.). After months of hard negotiations, our politicians in Washington delivered *bipartisan[213] legislation[214]* that will provide a better life experience to millions of people in our country. This legislation will go a long way toward closing the generation wealth gap by providing technology to poor people who live in remote areas. Policies like this change lives, and improve the world we live in. We could spend weeks celebrating this one piece of legislation. But we don't. Instead, the headline that day, on the same page, was

---

213. bipartisan: involving the agreement or cooperation of two political parties that usually oppose each other's policies
214. legislation: laws, considered collectively

"SCHOOL OFFICIAL USES RACIST MEME." The most unbelievable part of this is that the school official had been in good standing with the school for 35 years, a well-respected coach and leader in the community, and made a single mistake in a single email, for which the article goes on to say he apologized *profusely*[215] for and pledged to his community that he would improve his ways.The headline just as easily could have been "School Official Apologizes for Mistake, Seeks to Improve his Ways." Why do we not take advantage of the many opportunities we have to reinforce the good, instead of showcasing the bad? I am told that the people who run the media companies understand how vulnerable human beings are; meaning they know that we are hardwired to pay attention to messages that create strong emotions, such as fear, or lust, or desire or just to see good ole fashion "train wrecks" so they manipulate us; in order to ensure they attract enough eyeballs. I'm told it's all about the money. I don't want to believe that. Hopefully, you can see through this problem and address it for what it truly is.

I went to see Chris Rock, the famous comedian, in Boston a few nights after Will Smith slapped him in the face on national television. Most of his show was hilarious, I've always liked Chris Rock, and he was killing it. Then about three-quarters of the way through his act things took a turn. He basically said (I'm paraphrasing) "Man this country is so f'd up. We are done-America is Done..." and in the same breath he said something like "You Bostonians are a bunch of racists." From that moment on the crowd got quieter. People became tense and uneasy. We went from smiling and back-slapping each other to shifting in our seats and physically distancing from each other. It was so sad to see. As I sat there and witnessed the shift I felt certain that his material would be no less funny without the racist comments and that his ticket sales would not decrease one bit. I thought, at that moment the same way I have about so many other public officials, a sense of sadness and frustration and missed opportunity, and I wondered why entertainers like Mr. Rock don't consider what happens when they cross the line.

Chris Rock is a brilliant guy, certainly smart enough to know where the line is. He could have recognized that it was a racially mixed crowd that night who came out in Boston traffic, to

---

215. profusely: to a great degree; in large amounts

support him. We greeted the comedian with a long and gracious standing ovation which, at the start of the show he said "made him misty." His stuff was so funny, and he was doing so well.. but like everything else in life, he pushed too far. He had us in the palm of his hand. In that moment, as a celebrity, he could have used his status to join us together in solidarity as fellow human beings. He could have built a sense of shared trust in each other, as citizens, neighbors, and community members. Instead of reinforcing how good we can be, he chose to remind us of all our problems. Instead of helping to close the door on racism, he opened it further to all those who are on the edge of hate to hate. Instead of building on what we had- a sense of unity- he subtracted from it. We all left the joint feeling worse about our country and more divided by our race, than when we entered.

Whether it's our fascist politicians, our friends or family, comedians, or ourselves -we all create our false reality. We all let the cultural virus of casual ignorance infect us. We lull each other to sleep. We socialize with each other and bring each other down. The founders of our country gave us the First Amendment at a time when they each thought that we would learn how to use our rights and privileges as citizens of our newfound country responsibly, as a group of virtuous people. Today, we are a society defined by our lowest common denominator. We have chased our rights and privileges right into the toilet bowl. We have slowly but surely become Bob.

Learning how to use our freedoms in the manner our founding fathers intended, requires a level of thought and awareness that is not easily understood. Alexis De Tocqueville, the French philosopher who wrote extensively about America at the time of the formation of our union, and who was a great student of the American Constitution as well as the values the founders had in writing it, wrote "Nothing is more wonderful than the art of being free, but nothing is harder to learn how to use than freedom" (Metaxas, 2016, p. 1). I believe in freedom of expression as much as anyone, but if living in our society today has taught us anything, it is that not all expression is free. In fact, it comes at a great cost to society. We have come to believe that we are free to say and do whatever we want, but in reality, we are not.

In Massachusetts, we recently elected our first gay Governor, the first in the nation. She is modest and moderate so I like her and voted for her. However, I watched her acceptance speech. She said, "let my win be a lesson to every LGBTQIA+ person out there- that you can be whatever and whoever you want to be!" Now, I know she did not mean to do any harm. In fact, the opposite is true, I'm quite sure she means well. She wants to empower people who she feels could benefit from the message. But without some qualification, without some effort to reach the OTHER side- I'm afraid that she also conveys the same message to haters of the gay and lesbian community- that they too can be whatever and whoever they want to be. In America today, for every person who read the morning newspaper with glee that the first openly lesbian woman had become a Governor, about half of all other people in America sadly *lamented*[216] the moment. If Maura Healy caused 5 MILLION gay and lesbian people to feel empowered, she also caused 5 MILLION other people to raise their mostly masculine fists against her and her ideas.

So, you must be wondering, how do people speak up for what they believe, without further driving people apart? How do we make change in society without causing great division? How do we make all this confusion with politics go away? This goes to the delicacy of it all. The founders of our country had the answer. The underlying foundation for our whole system of government was that we needed each citizen to place the concept of being an American, ahead of everything else. We can and should be proud of who we are, gay lesbian, straight, white, black, brown, so long as we never forget that we are citizens FIRST. We all have the right to *discriminate*[217]. If we don't like tomatoes we don't have to try them. Similarly, there are people we just don't want to hang out with. We have this right too, but as citizens, we can only take our discrimination so far. If you want to live in a cave and not participate in society, then you don't have to play by societal rules. Go live in a cave. That freedom you have, but once you pass back into a shared reality, your reality is just that, it's shared. **We are not free to be whoever and whatever we want to be in a shared society**. To make it all work requires this level of thought.

As I've said, being a good citizen is a far higher bar than being a

---

216.. lament: a passionate expression of grief or sorrow
217. discriminate: having or showing refined taste or good judgment

good person. We do not have many bad people in society… but we do have a lot of bad citizens.

In closing this chapter, I often wonder what would happen if people like Chris Rock and Kid Rock would consider their obligations as citizens as an opportunity rather than a burden. The two of these guys are probably friends- but nobody would know it. As we know, people tend to fill the void of information with our worst assumptions about each other. Can you imagine all the good they could do by changing their acts just a little bit, so as to help us see through our myths rather than playing on our fears, and creating our false reality? Haven't we all had enough of this chaotic and stressful existence? Isn't it time we end this hate train? Don't we want our kids to grow up in a better world? I think we all want off this ride. So this goes out to Mr. Kid Rock and Mr. Chris Rock- Please help us. You could literally save millions of lives by just paying a little more attention and doing your part.

The people who have gained an audience could help us most. They could reinforce the simple principles which could bring about incredible change. That we are not free to live without care and compassion for our fellow man. When we strive to be free of all empathy, care, and concern for other people or other groups, we stop living the life intended for us. Whether by intentional act or by careless omission, when we fail to outwardly demonstrate empathy and understanding for the other side of an issue; when we don't celebrate our diversity and differences in a similar sense of appreciating or loving all of God's creatures; when we lock into self-protection mode for ourselves and our families, and we lose sight of the bigger picture, our good intentions for our family, ourselves, or our group, backfire on us.

What about you, my young reader? Now that you see the noise and confusion for what it truly is- something we are all contributing to, without really thinking about it, will you do your part to help us end the myths which have forever kept us divided? Will you help us create a better reality, the one that was truly intended for us by nature? If you are one of those kids who has guided yourself to having true friends at this time in your life – congratulations! Next time at school, please look around you and think about those kids who may not be feeling as comfortable as you. Maybe a kid who doesn't look like you.

Someone who seems to be struggling- You know who they are. The kids who are being left out or bullied. You are old enough to realize that some of these kids will get so far down in the dumps, that they can end up doing terrible things to themselves and others. Now that you know, will you extend a kind word, or friendship, to a person who needs it? Please don't stand by and watch someone get left out, or mistreated. If you see bullying occurring on social media, end it. Don't let peer pressure, which comes from your dumb elephant brain stop you from speaking up. If you feel it is wrong it is wrong. Listen to how people talk to each other. If you feel they are belittling the other person, don't let a terrible communicator rule the moment. Don't laugh at jokes that are hurtful. When you are in a public setting you are acting as a citizen to a shared community. Remember that 90% of the people around you know what immoral behaviors look like. When the time and place reveals itself to you (and it will) find courage in the 90% rule, but be patient and stay modest, keep listening to the other side, and try to understand where they are coming from. Face your fears and be the bigger person. You can make a bigger impact than you realize. The stronger you can be on this issue, the more successful you will become, in many aspects of your life.

Chapter 13: Making Change

Certainly, a brighter future is one where we all realize the part we play in creating our reality, however, the fact is -we can't change Bob. Sorry if it took me so long to confirm that. Our beloved broncos, ostriches, Uncle and Aunt D's, are too far down the road, and their belief system is not consistent with the natural laws. We are never going to change them. They are going to die off before you do and we can say a friendly goodbye to them at their funerals. We need to focus intently on the education of young people. It is our only chance.

Our new normal is not some flavor of the month moral panic-it's a lot larger than that. I hope that you agree that we are going to have to take a whole new approach in order to break this pattern that we find ourselves locked in. We are going to have to take what we say to each other a lot more seriously. Every word matters. Politics, like business, is not something you joke about or laugh about. There is really not that much to laugh about when it comes to politics or business. It's called work for a reason. Yet most of us continue to joke around about politics. We need to understand that when we laugh at bad jokes or make stupid and careless remarks about our political opponents or our President, that we make our problems worse.

We cannot separate ourselves from the way other people act. When someone calls our President an A-Hole, it makes us all A-Holes. Each time we witness someone doing something or saying something that makes our stomach turn, we need to be blaming ourselves for their continued lack of grace and dignity. I know this seems like advanced work, and it is. It's not easy to understand that we need to take a bite out of those rotten tomatoes from time to time to play our part as citizens, but this is exactly what is required of us if we want to reach the goals set forth in this book. The fate of the human race depends on it. When my son John or Mikey tells me that I need to lighten up and that we will never be able to get enough people to pay this much attention, I must sternly disagree with them. Young people are capable of change.

Change will take time- of course. In fact, as long as it takes for our myths to form and grab hold of our society, we should expect that it takes equally as long for us to dispel the myths- this is consistent with nature's rules about balance, moderation, and modesty. We cannot enter a room and demand change and behave like we have all the answers. But what we can do is trust in the 90 percent rule, that 90% of the people in any room we enter feel the same way we do. We can use this rule as a source of confidence. Because it is truth derived from natural law. As such it is a truth that you can rely on.

You are going to have to figure out how to speak to one another. What we currently lack is some organization or structure, an improved process for dealing with our most radical voices.

For 27 years, I worked in construction, and there were very strict building codes and regulations that I had to work under. There were building officials from multiple departments of local, state, and federal government who had jurisdiction over my job sites. My jobs were often delayed or stopped due to their interpretations of the rules. Without progress on our jobs, we didn't get paid. The building officials were the law, and we followed the rules. Let's stop for a moment and think about the situation we are in. People are constantly inciting other people to violence against fellow Americans, and there are no rules in place to stop this. But at the same time, I can't complete my construction project because a building official woke up on the wrong side of the bed, or because his Egg McMuffin was cold. Today we intervene in people's lives in the wrong things. We can do so much better.

There are many hard questions you need to answer such as: How great should the divide be, in terms of how fellow Americans experience life? There will always be differences in life experience: How wide will you allow it to be? We will always, to some degree, have the haves and the have-nots in our society. What should be acceptable levels of "winning" and "losing" at the American life experience? How much should the winners care about those who are losing? And should the winners be forced by elected officials to give back – how much? How tolerant can we expect those befallen with bad luck and misfortune to be of those who seem to be having all of the luck in America? How do we get people with different life experiences to live in harmony with one another? How much time should we spend recognizing past wrongs such as slavery, and how do we get all Americans to agree about such things? We will always have to debate who the real victims are in life. Government will never be all things for all people. Political issues will always be hard. There will always be people who question the issues of equality, access, inclusion, and fairness and these circumstances will never change. So where does that leave us?

We cannot regulate what people say, but what if we were to learn how to communicate effectively with one another? Isn't that all we need? These questions could be answered and people could co-exist peacefully, even happily. Life is all about trade-offs. So isn't all that matters is the process of how we arrive at those trade-offs? It's the process of how we disagree that is far more important than the underlying issues themselves. If people trust the process, they will trust the result. If we trust we were fairly treated in the process of disagreement, then we do not get overly worked up about the result. The details of the underlying things we must debate are not important. We cannot begin to get to those issues, without first understanding that we share a common identity and a purpose. People cannot communicate unless they have some type of relationship, which establishes a bit of trust. We need to be on the same team before pulling in the same direction. People who do not form relationships in advance of trying to work through issues will always struggle. You will see this playing out in your classes and on your teams. The same is true with our government. We cannot possibly answer any of these questions until we regain some trust in one another. The key is to learn how to have healthy conflict. We need to figure out how to communicate with people with whom we disagree, without hating each other. All we can do is engage people in the process of being citizens. We need to focus less on reaching an agreement about things and much more focus on **HOW to disagree.**

Therefore, I am asking, and suggesting that you help design, build, and maintain a more intelligent, well-mannered way to disagree. Grass Roots, local organizations, with a singular mission: To discuss the meaning of "free speech".

We can develop a code together. We might call it an American Decency and Communication Code, like a building code it will be built at local levels, facilitated by small associations, with participation from a wide sampling of citizens, and coordinated state-to-state across the country. I believe we need to create such a platform with a singular goal of discussing where we are to draw the lines. We could provide educational materials through the local council of volunteers. It's best if it doesn't start out as being regulated by the National government. We need to start off slowly, rebuilding trust in smaller groups. So we start in our local towns. Then it will spread to cities. Then to state and then in time as we build back trust of one another- using the tools in this book and the many other books just like it, we can consider how we formalize it. You might give the process a name. For example: "The American code of civic behavior" but be sure to arrive at the name in a democratic fashion. Don't come in hot and start telling people what to do. The mission is to discuss the rules- and focus on HOW that discussion must go, instead of a focus on the ultimate rules themselves. Remember that some people will freak out because we are coming up with a new council- that smells very "government like", but if you just keep faith in the 90% rule you will be great.

Keep your eye on the ball here. We are not trying to grow the size of government- it's just the opposite. The idea is to be able to improve the way we disagree about things, with the **goal of being able to shrink the size of a central government.** The only way we can put power in the hands of the people is to be able to learn together and rebuild trust in one another. We need to OPEN the DEBATE to what decency and American values look like. We need to do away with the word Politics altogether and replace it with a discussion about what it means to be a good citizen. Without trampling on individual rights, and without expanding the size of government, we can form local councils with the sole purpose to get in a room together and discuss the rights and duties of citizenship. We need to recodify and re-define our words together! Only then we will reestablish trust in our laws.

Nobody is going to jail for saying really stupid stuff. But as I've said many times, we need some sources of authority in our lives to hold each other accountable to basic principles of courtesy and respect, befitting another citizen. When placed in a context of considering what our alternatives are- I hope that we will prioritize this effort. When Bob at the driving range tells me that he wants to shoot our President, we could start by sending a letter with educational materials to Bob's home, asking him to consider a different approach. We could leave educational materials in the local library for Bob, such as the rules of Ben Franklin's clubs, and the reasons behind those rules, as well we could show him the result, which was American democracy. Democracy needs to be taught. We cannot just allow people to trample all over our democracy without making some effort to educate them. There are ways to educate people. If Bob was unable to read, our local council would provide him free literacy education.

These councils will not be perfect, because people are imperfect. We can figure out the details together. We need to let people be whatever type of person they want. Remember we can only judge people for how they are as citizens, not as human beings. Opinions will vary greatly. But when a group of imperfect people gather around in person to discuss their imperfections- the most amazing things happen. We begin to regain trust in humanity. We can't do this over the phone, or the Internet. The work of citizenship only happens in person.

Chapter 14: Race

I want to say a few things about the politicized issue of race. The last thing we want to do is avoid our most difficult issues. If we are serious about creating a more just society we need to face up to reality. I am going to cut to the chase about race and make this statement. Our history is *replete*[218] with facts about the long-term effects of slavery on black Americans. Therefore, any denial of slavery's impacts is plain stupid... Oh wait a second- I know that I just said that we can't go around calling people stupid, so let me restate that. Any denial that slavery existed or that it has not had negative side effects for black people in this country is reserved for the most closed-minded among us. I hope that was a little better?

Let me put this differently. If you are one to think any less of people because of the color of their skin, you are mistaken. Your belief system is wrong. The chances are that if you hold this belief, and treat people differently because of their ethnicity or skin color during the course of your life, you are not going to do very well in your life. It's also likely that you will be going to a place that resembles hell when you die. But don't take my word for any of this, I'm just the guy who read a bunch of books, and who found the natural law. Sorry to have to start this chapter with a threat, but we really need to be able to talk about reality, not skewed versions of reality. So let's do this for a minute.

As of 2019, the average white household in our country has eight times more money than the average black family. (Moss et al., 2020). Abe Lincoln was murdered on April 14, 1865, by a racist. This was only two years after Lincoln had issued the *Emancipation Proclamation* [219] which ended the practice of slavery. He was replaced by a very ordinary man named Andrew Johnson who went about reversing many of the laws that would give former slaves lots of land and other rights which had been

218. replete: filled or well-supplied with something
219. emancipation proclamation: the proclamation issued by President Lincoln on September 22, 1862, that freed the people held as slaves in those territories still in rebellion against the Union from January 1, 1863, forward.

promised to blacks by their emancipation. After the end of the Civil War, the Southern Homestead Act intended to provide land to newly Emancipated African Americans... this land act benefited white families and excluded black families. (Merrit, 2016) The Homestead Acts gave millions of white families plots of land in America, while black people were not included in this opportunity. Generations of black people have lacked equal access to wealth and education ever since.

For many years I've been involved in two organizations in my town which address issues of race. We meet periodically to talk about all issues concerning our communities, including topics concerning race relations. We often take long walks in the woods together, wondering, laughing, and smiling with each other, why we have to talk about race, or skin color, at all. But that's us. Of course, there are times when the work gets very real, and looking into the faces of my longtime black friends on the board, you realize that understanding each other fully is not possible. Recently, I've made some bold statements for which there was wide disagreement. Because I am a white male, the reason in me tells me that it may not be entirely fair for me to take any strong position. It certainly seems daring for me to talk about the sensitive issues of race and skin color in our country, given I was never enslaved. That we are having the difficult conversations to begin with is one of the things that I hope you will take away from this chapter. I want to point out one topic that we've been discussing regarding race relations in our community.

On a recent walk, I questioned if I am truly colorblind, that is if I have equal respect, true love, and admiration for every human being regardless of their skin color, is that enough, or whether I need to go further than that? I am open to learning about how to be "anti-racist", which is a call to be more than colorblind. I understand that being anti-racist asks us to make a proactive effort to repair the injustices done in the past. I'm happy to go further, I told my friends, but I also said that I believe that those among them who are asking me to go further may be making a big mistake.

It seems to me that we keep making the same mistake, regardless of which side we are on, of pushing a little too hard. Similar to when Chris Rock pushes his material too far or when Kid Rock pushes his lyrics too far. I believe the few who are pushing too hard are tainting the message for the many. Take the issue of reparations. The idea of government forcing current citizens to make payments for the wrongs of our distant past. I realize why many black, brown, and native American people ask those of us who have not been through what they have, to never forget the injustices and indecencies which they have suffered, and to make certain reparations. It's a fair request, one that doesn't ask too much of us- if we were a deep and critical-thinking society, but therein lies the problem. We are not- at least not yet.

And I am sorry about this. But it's as if, with all the other issues of political correctness in the news, all at one time, the issue of reparations has been too much for ordinary people to handle. I know if I were black what I would be thinking... "Well that's too bad for the average white person, I don't need to apologize for anything, white people have had it SO good for all these years, while my people have suffered." I can understand that and I wish things were different. But those of us really concerned about these things, we need to find a different way out of our cycle. As it stands today, our culture is just too ordinary. We need to face up to our reality and understand how ordinary we are. We are not even close to advanced enough to handle repayments.

Our current approach is just not working. There is just no denying that a focus on our past, in the form of strict attention to issues of systemic racism and critical race theory has been a deep source of polarization. Many believe that the BLM movement was a necessary movement that was effective. Others believe that it ended up not creating the type of changes that its proponents, like me, intended. I'm afraid, like so many other named social movements and activists' efforts that are well intended- the slogan itself- "BLM " came to be yet another casualty in our war of extremes.

I once tried to explain the concept of White Privilege to Meg (short for Maggie or Margaret), the person who cuts my hair, and she almost cut my ear off. She held the scissors to my ear lobe and said, "Don't you DARE call me privileged. Me and my husband do all we can to put food on the table. Nobody has ever done me a favor, not the government- nobody!" Meg is like most other humans. She tends to group all the issues together and get caught up in her impression of things. She basically shaved my right eyebrow off when I told her that I thought Joe Biden was doing a pretty good job. This is another example of how much terminology matters. I almost learned the hard way.

At this point, I would respectfully ask that we use more foresight than hindsight. I want to ask people to consider how it has been shortsighted of us to try to fix things all at once. I would also ask those people, who were victims, to consider that class and financial status is a better proxy than race, long term, to ensure equal justice and opportunities moving forward. Kindly consider that Government programs are designed to consider a person's economic status and to look after those who cannot take care of themselves. This includes the poor, the sick, the disabled, the very young, the very old. If or when more non-whites fall into any of these categories, (which they do because of the lasting effects of slavery) they do receive the bulk of benefits from our policies- as they should. All I'm asking is that we don't push too far on each other. We are only human after all.

I would also ask that we let go of any grudges that anyone might feel for wrongs done in the past. Holding grudges is why we have two sides that continually blame the other side for being morally corrupt. In order to break the pattern we are in, we need to play "the long game," and think deeply about what we can do in the future to create a more tolerant and accepting human race. We have been hating each other over the issue of slavery for years with no movement on either side. It's proving too hard to move backward. We are having a hard enough time moving forward. This policy effort to make up for past wrongs as well-intentioned as they have, respectfully in my opinion, has thrown us way out of equilibrium. I am quite certain that the calling for reparations is a form of extreme activism that is backfiring on us.

Change as we've said in the last chapter will take time. Let us not continue to make the same mistake of pretending people are ready for change when they are not. We need to do a better job of preparing our young people to be tolerant. It will take time before a future generation breaks free from the chains of our own ordinariness, and becomes extraordinary, through education, but we have one reason to be hopeful- Among a group of third- or fourth-graders you couldn't find one racist. They wouldn't know what it is.

In conclusion, if I believe that if I am a person, or you are, who can be sensitive to issues of race and am willing to continue to learn, then that should be enough. If we focus on educating all young adults to develop the prefrontal cortex and to use the "breakthrough" psychologies discussed in Chapter Ten, a future generation of like-minded adults will come together to finally eliminate our terrible disagreements and hate over issues of race. Each of us can be the spark that lights the flame of goodness in others and by doing so we will slowly change all of human nature for the better. This was the supreme creator's plan all along!

Chapter 15: Final Thoughts

When I was seven or eight years old, (the late 70s) my father would often take me to a horse racing and betting track. You heard that right. It was in East Boston, called Suffolk Downs. The track was a gritty place. The thousands of cigarette butts on the ground is not something an eight-year-old soon forgets, but that isn't what I remember most about the track… Far from it. What I remember is how my father interacted with so many different types of people, and no matter where they came from, what they looked like, or how they dressed, everyone was treated with the same amount of respect. To me, everyone at the track seemed to share the same values. Maybe it's because my dad preferred to sit with the underpaid horse handlers and hourly workers rather than the more deep-pocketed fellow horse owners, but like I said, it didn't seem to matter- everyone blended together. What I remember most about Suffolk, even more than the people, or how quickly a kid my age could lose six bucks, was the race course itself and how *impeccably*[220] clean they kept it.

After each race, these massive green tractors, three or four of them, would round the course several times to clean its surface deeply. The tractors' sweeping apparatus created these intense grooves that were perfectly *symmetrical*[221] and gave the horses a clean run up the track and to the finish line. The preparation process signified for me a great respect that was shown for the runners, the *majestic* horses, and the jockeys that guided them along their journey. There was something *sacred* about it. Those images of the track never left me and at that time, all seemed right with the world.

Fast forward a few years to when I sat down to write a birthday card to my son. I found myself very confused and frustrated as the world seemed to be changing in ways that nobody could understand. Almost everyone seemed to agree that things had become very weird, even scary, but yet nobody could quite put a finger on what "it" was. It felt as if the world was spinning at an

---

220. impeccably: in accordance with the highest standards; faultlessly
221. symmetrical: made up of exactly similar parts facing each other or around an axis; showing symmetry

unstoppable rate of speed and that we had become unglued from anything- truth or reality- that had formerly held our society together. Families, groups, friendships, even once respectful opponents… all torn apart by some indescribable force.

As a parent and a first-time teacher being faced with questions about "it", I was at a complete loss. "It" was weighing on my students' minds and I didn't know what to say. I couldn't even finish a simple birthday card for my son. It was at that moment that I made a decision. I would go looking for it, in order to make some sense of it, and to hopefully help my kids and their kids not have to contend with whatever the hell it was, any longer. My burning desire to find "it" took me to a most logical place, but one that I hadn't visited in years -the library. What I found there *astonished*[222] me.

Over a few months of searching, with staff wondering how crazy I was, I had my first epiphany. I found that there were thousands of people far smarter than I, who had beaten me to "it". Every book, every author, regardless of time, seemed to speak about something called the natural law, but all did so in different ways. This realization ignited me further and gave me reason for optimism. After a few years, now totally mesmerized by the possibility of salvation in finding an actual source of truth- in a world that seemed to have lost understanding of it -the library walls finally spoke to me and revealed "it" to me.

Truth and reality for humankind is determined by nature, and its laws are amazingly simple:

> 1. We each have a deep well of goodness in us; we are born with major gifts but we have to use -em, or we lose- em.

> 2. The virtue we gain is meant to be shared with others because we are all born by the same creator.

These laws have been established over the course of thousands of years, and in many ways have been proven by the miracle of education and modern science. Hopefully, the totally nonsensical, illogical, and divided times that we have all been

---

222. astonishing: extremely surprising or impressive; amazing

living through, are the best and last proof that we need to see the light. That the natural laws are real. Truly real. I've tried everything in my power, short of the ole "pinky swear" to prove that these laws are true, and will continue to be true forever. Nobody can or will prove anything differently.

Because these laws are our reality, when we detach, it can only follow that we begin to believe things that are not true or real, and we live according to a distorted reality. Too many of us go through life not fully actualizing our gifts, and not trusting in cosmopolitanism. This is why we have an underperforming society. We will either adapt to these laws or continue to suffer the consequences. You may not think that people are punished by not following the natural laws, but we are. If what we are seeing currently in our society is not a form of punishment, I give up.

It should not surprise any of us to learn that the force that has been punishing us is nature itself. All one has to do is watch a few nature shows on Nat Geo or Netflix, or even better, go stand on a mountaintop similar to the one on the cover of this book, and you will understand just how powerful our natural world is. Only our fighting against a force this large could produce the sheer chaos that we have seen play out in the last few years or account for the many years of war and conflict across the globe.

There is a reason why natural law works so well. It grounds us in a universal truth about people, that we are good. We all want to achieve and make ourselves proud. We all seek happiness over sadness. We all seek the affection of our families and friends. None of us were born to be lazy cheats. None of us want assistance and handouts from our wealthier, neighbors who worked harder than us. Natural law says that we all just want a fair shake. Without this fundamental belief in the goodness of mankind, we don't stand a chance. Natural law could give us a universal religion. It is what the founders of our country relied on to build our government, but we tend to forget things. In America, because we don't teach or follow the natural laws, we allow false myths about people to creep in. For example, the notion that poor people and those in need only exist to peer over at the wealthy in disgust and want to take their stuff. This is a distortion of reality. God didn't make people like this. Yet because of our own carelessness, we have locked ourselves into the wrong assumptions about people. This keeps us stuck in a spin cycle of suck, and mediocrity. Everyone blames each other, instead of coming together to rally around the real truth. People do not want government assistance- they simply need some assistance at times in their lives. People get sick and they get old- And sometimes they need a little help.

Ninety percent of us know this. There is truth and right and wrong in this world **precisely because** man has a special gift of knowing it. Hopefully, what we have learned together in this book, is all the reasons why some of us deviate from it. The reason why we fail to rally around the natural laws is because they are packed with counterintuitive truths.

It's hard to believe that what we say matters that much to the lives of people whom we do not even know or that we have to work so hard as individual citizens to advance humankind **or** be a cause of its destruction. It's hard to believe that so many fine people born into the world can have so much capacity for greatness, but yet turn into such buttholes. That so many of us lose the battle with our divided minds, and become unbalanced- either too far left or too far right, too conservative or too liberal. It's hard to believe that the uncaring attitude of so few, becomes the uncaring attitude of so many. It's also hard to believe that it's our failure to pay attention to mental health issues of all our citizens (at a young age), that we end up with millions of narcissists running around with too much self-confidence who are walking all over millions of super empaths who have too little. It's hard to believe that people becoming extreme in one direction or the other is the cause of all dysfunction in human affairs, but it's true. It's hard to believe that if we cut off extremism we will cut off hate. It may be hard for anyone to accept that the powers that be actually spoke to me in the library that night, or that the powers can speak to any one of us. It's hard to believe that our purpose is to carry out our creator's intentions, and that is how things work down here. Yet this, all true- because it's all according to nature.

I would have never found these counterintuitive truths unless I returned to reading. When we go to the library, this is an act of seeking wisdom, and this is what the natural law asks of us. To keep our eyes open and seek knowledge. We cannot possibly understand the brilliance of man unless we read. It seems all of the books in the library cannot do one thing: they cannot get us to read them. Unless we get back to reading and writing, which are the tools of wisdom seekers, and practitioners of the natural law, we will fail to self master, continue to wallow in our own ordinariness, and remain blind as a society to the destiny that could otherwise be available to us. Your generation will have to return to reading to be successful.

I want to make you a promise- if you read and learn about the people who shaped America you will find reason to believe there is a consistency of goodness in the thousands of remarkable thinkers that have gone before us, and if you are one to think that you want to question their goodness or what they stood for that is okay, it is very important that you do that! But please don't do this blindly. I'm not asking you to believe me. All I am asking is that you take the time to learn about their lives. The more I have read about the lives of our past heroes, men and women of all types, I have been absolutely convinced of the goodness of mankind.

There are thousands of pages of letters from our founding fathers in our Library of Congress, but only a very small percentage of our society is reading them. There is so much about our country that people do not know. Just the other day, I found a penny and looked closely at it. Pictured here, it says "In God We Trust", and on the other side "E Pluribus Unum" which I later learned is the motto of the United States. "Out of Many- One". The truth is that there could be a book written, every day, and only about how much good people do for each other. For example just today I read that there were over 200,000 families who volunteered to take in refugee families from the war-torn region of Ukraine and that Americans had raised over 275 Million dollars to ensure basic human rights for people who have been impacted by yet another group of people violating natural laws, and becoming unglued. (Kight, 2023). Today, I learned that in my state of Massachusetts, taxpayers spend 45,000,000 Million dollars per month, helping families with young children who live below the poverty line, with shelter and other necessities. Yet few of us would know this for all the reasons we've discussed.

For way too long we have been lying to ourselves. We have taken the most convenient path, and have made just about every mistake there is to make. We are living in a false reality because we are not doing the work we need to do as a society.

I'm asked all the time these simple questions:

> 1. If kids don't have good parenting, how can we expect them to stay healthy and not turn against society?

> 2. If kids grow up in poverty how can we expect them to be well-adjusted, patient, and to contribute to society?

The answer to both of these questions is the same- I don't! I do not expect people who grow up in poverty or with poor parenting to have peace and fulfillment in their lives and to contribute to cosmopolitanism. You shouldn't either!

When kids are not getting the parenting they need, we, the people, the community, friends, neighbors, places of worship, and **YES- The government** needs to fill in and provide that support. We need to help each other. **We are the government.** We cannot expect poor people to go along living half an existence and to be happy, helpful citizens. We need to help every American child win the battle with their divided mind, feel like somebody, to feel included, and valued. We need to create a village of support and treat all kids in America as our own. If we continue to fail to see our reality for what it is, we will continue along the same littered road of myths and falsehoods that have kept us divided. The fact that we fool ourselves into thinking that people who live in poverty, or without proper support, will not grow up to hate and kill other people, or to bring society down, is just downright silly, but more importantly, it is inconsistent with nature's laws, and that is why we continue to suffer.

I want to say one last thing about that natural law. Nowhere does the natural law talk about individual freedoms, it only talks about obligations. This is what some of our greatest philosophers over the course of history have tried to remind us of. When JFK said those famous words at his inauguration on January 20th, 1961 "Ask not what your country can do for you, Ask what you can do for your country"- he spoke of personal impositions, not of personal freedoms. In 1906, Theodore Roosevelt, a deep thinker, and our 26th President said that "The foundation stone of national life is, and ever must be, the high individual character of the average citizen". (Roosevelt, n.d.).

So now it's your turn. You can either embrace the advice given by "all the books in the library" and supported by modern science, to create the peace and welfare intended for all of us. Or you can continue to *wallow*[223] in a distorted reality, continuing to fight with your fellow human beings, "*condemned*[224] to mutual incomprehension" (as now our favorite psychologist, Dr. Haidt would say). All young minds have to do, to improve our America is to do a better job of understanding human nature. When you do this, you will do a better job of managing our freedoms. You hold the fate of the human race in your hands. No pressure.

I want to end on the best news of all. There is a great payoff for doing all this. It's that little thing called happiness. Your being involved in politics and government may seem like a real hassle and a thankless situation right now. It may not seem like the cool thing to do, but it will be one of the most worthwhile and fulfilling things that you will ever do in your life. When we see ourselves as someone who is a part of something larger than ourselves, we live with more fulfillment and happiness.

Remember, there is nothing more advanced than we are, except only who or what created us. Our creator has given us a great capacity to learn. Keep learning, set up a system of education and training so that all Americans understand how to remain balanced, and your generation can truly change the world forever. And if that isn't enough for you, you should know that the work which keeps us mentally strong and to be a good citizen just so happens to also be the stuff of happiness. You're sitting on the sidelines will feel as badly to you as it sounds. Haters are not happy. It's because they have become detached from the path intended for all of us humans.

Many of the world's deepest thinkers have argued that happiness

---

223. wallow: roll about or lie relaxed in mud or water,
224. condemned: sentenced to a particular punishment, especially death

and living with "virtue" are linked. **Socrates said, "The good life, the beautiful life, and the just life are the same."** Philosopher Rabryinth Tagore said, **"I slept and dreamt that life was joy. I awoke and saw that life was service. I acted and behold, service was Joy".** I am pleased to report that this is consistent with my life experience.

This book started out as an advice book for my son, so I want to close it in that fashion, with some final words of advice which help summarize what I have learned and what I want you to know. First, the great Dale Carnegie said, <u>"There are no neutral exchanges in life, you either make a person feel better or worse for having spoken to them." (Carnegie, 2012)</u> Always try to see where another person is coming from, and remember- look deeply for the good in others, and affirm the good in them even if it's only something small. Look for the small sparks, and you will ignite them. Do not place people in a category or a bucket, based on a message that you may get on Snapchat. Carnegie also said, "You can make more friends in two months by becoming more interested in other people than you can in two years by trying to get people interested in you" (Carnegie, 2012, p. Intro) So ease up on the selfies. Ask questions, be curious. Inquire with people as to what is going on in their lives.

"When you look at your life as a trip from humility to knowledge and back again, you are sure to always fly over Centerville." That is something I came up with, and I'm glad to offer it here near the end of my book because it goes to the essence of what I believe in. I've had some confident opinions in this book. I've only done this in the context of our world being so messed up for so long. The fact is, there is no substitute for humility. The more you observe the many wonders which are beyond your control, the more you demonstrate, to your peers, or your employer, or to your future voters (assuming some of you will run for office. And I hope that you do) that you can become the person who can solve for what is unknowable. Only a person who is intellectually humble can solve for the most complicated of all tasks, that thing which is called *ordered liberty*[225]. Faking a bit of humility from time to time works just as well, even if you are certain of things! Understand your vulnerability and be open to showing it- This will serve you well.

---

225. ordered liberty: freedom limited by the need for order in society

One last thing before I close. In my experience in life, there are choices that are put to us that we had no role in creating, and it therefore can seem awfully unfair that we are presented with them at all. Most of these choices can be a real hassle, with seemingly no good options. I contend that it is these choices, those that should not have been put to us but yet we have to make nonetheless that best define the character of a man or woman. The health of your own family, and the destiny of our society, depends on each of us making the right choice in these situations. These are the ones that will test your ability and understanding of the natural laws.

I wanted to share a picture of our family in the winner's circle at Suffolk Downs in 1977, that's me in the puffy tan jacket, and a photo of me with my dad who is holding a trophy (below).

Of course, like anyone, my father enjoyed winning more than losing. In fact, he once mentioned to me that one of his goals was to win the Kentucky Derby. For a long time, I thought that this aspiration of his may be his way of becoming a "somebody". I mean we all want to be a "somebody". He never got a horse to that big race, and in fact, he would lose many more races than he would win- but when my father died I learned that he had given a large portion of the money he had earned in his life to the Massachusetts General Hospital and other charities. In doing so, he proved to me that in order to be a "somebody" you only need to care about everybody. I hope that you never lose sight of this fact.

It took me a few years to finally come to realize what the noise and confusion my students felt was all about, and why so many young adults today remain wary of growing up in the USA. Us adults have littered the racecourse in front of you and in doing so have greatly disrespected a whole generation of young Americans. I can hardly think of anything worse than the feeling of being disrespected. Adults should be here to help you make your life a bit easier, not to make things more difficult for you, but that is what we have done. I hope this book has armed you with the ability to see through the garbage, the myths, and the bullshit, that we have carelessly and wrongfully thrown out in front of you. You deserve better, and now you know better.

To Mikey, John, Katie, and my beloved readers, please know that I love and care for you deeply. I ask you to care about being a good citizen and place this above everything else in your own development, it will not fail you. If you never stop seeing your potential or believing in the potential of others, you will actualize your gifts, fill your life with meaning, and live a most rewarding existence. When each of us chooses to live more intentionally and guided by the right basis of knowledge we will slowly bring an end to extremism and eventually turn all of humanity for the better. Your generation can and will finally end terrible disagreement and hate forever. Find your spirit. Stay the course. You can do it!

Glossary

Introduction

1. aberration: a departure from what is normal, usual, or expected, typically one that is unwelcome

2. civil: courteous and polite

3. Dignity: the state or quality of being worthy of honor or respect

4. Respect: due regard for the feelings, wishes, rights, or traditions of others virtue: behavior showing high moral standards

5. morality: the principles concerning the distinction between right and wrong or good and bad behaviors

6. Revelation: a surprising and previously unknown fact, especially one that is made known in a dramatic way

7. Civilization: the stage of human social and cultural development and organization that is considered most advanced

8. Theatrical: exaggerated and excessively dramatic

9. Unconventional: not based on or conforming to what is generally done or believed

10. epidemic: a widespread occurrence of an infectious disease in a community at a particular time

11. self-righteous: having or characterized by a certainty, especially an unfounded one, that one is totally correct or morally superior

12. politician: a person who is professionally involved in

politics, especially as a holder of or a candidate for an elected office

Chapter 1

13. incontrovertible: not able to be denied or disputed

14. revolutionary: involving or causing a complete or dramatic change

15. incomprehensible: not able to be understood; not intelligible

16. genetics: the study of heredity and the variation of inherited characteristics

17. altruistic: showing a disinterested and selfless concern for the well-being of others; unselfish

18. empathy: the ability to understand and share the feelings of another

Chapter 2

19. vigilant: keeping careful watch for possible danger or difficulties

20. doozy: something outstanding or unique of its kind

21. metaphor: a figure of speech in which a word or phrase is applied to an object or action to which it is not literally applicable

22. profound: of a state, quality, or emotion) very great or intense

23. posthoc: after the fact and made-up

24. citizenship: the position or status of being a citizen of a

particular country

25. freedoms: the power or right to act, speak, or think as one wants without hindrance or restraint

26. regulation: a rule or directive made and maintained by an authority

27. succumb: fail to resist pressure, temptation or some other negative force

28. suboptimal: of less than the highest standard or quality

29. degenerate: having lost the physical, mental, or moral qualities considered normal and desirable; showing evidence of decline.

30. ignorant: lacking knowledge or awareness in general; uneducated or unsophisticated

Chapter 3

31. spirit: the nonphysical part of a person which is the seat of emotions and character; the soul

32. antidote: a medicine taken or given to counteract a particular poison

33. cliche: a phrase or opinion that is overused and betrays a lack of original thought

34. jovial: cheerful and friendly

35. thesaurus: a book or electronic resource that lists words in groups of synonyms and related concepts

36. liberated: (of a place or people) freed from imprisonment, slavery, or enemy occupation

37. concentration camp: a place where large numbers of people,

especially political prisoners or members of persecuted minorities, are deliberately imprisoned in a relatively small area with inadequate facilities, sometimes to provide forced labor or to await mass execution. The term is most strongly associated with the several hundred camps established by the Nazis in Germany and occupied Europe in 1933–45, among the most infamous being Dachau, Belsen, and Auschwitz

38. de-loused: to remove lice from

39. epitome: a person or thing that is a perfect example of a particular quality or type

40. alchemy: a seemingly magical process of transformation, creation, or combination

41. by-product: an incidental or secondary product made in the manufacture or synthesis of something else

42. humility: a modest or low view of one's own importance; humbleness

43. resolute: admirably purposeful, determined, and unwavering

44. grace: simple elegance or refinement of movement

45. politeness: behavior that is respectful and considerate of other people

46. Disposition: a person's inherent qualities of mind and character

47. supernatural: (of a manifestation or event) attributed to some force beyond scientific understanding or the laws of nature.

48. toxic: very harmful or unpleasant in a pervasive or insidious way.

49. Polarizing: divide or cause to divide into two sharply contrasting groups or sets of opinions or beliefs.

Chapter 4

50. Perplexity: a complicated or baffling situation or thing

51. contradiction: a combination of statements, ideas, or features of a situation that are opposed to one another

52. infatuated: possessed with an intense but short-lived passion or admiration for someone

53. insurmountable: too great to be overcome

54. ethics: moral principles that govern a person's behavior or the conduct of an activity.

55. customary: according to the customs or usual practices associated with a particular society, place, or set of circumstances.

56. etiquette: the customary code of polite behavior in society or among members of a particular profession or group.

57. assimilation: the process of taking in and fully understanding information or ideas

58. ostracized: exclude (someone) from a society or group

59. prudence: acting with or showing care and thought for the future

60. logic: reasoning conducted or assessed according to strict principles of validity

61. fraternity: a group of people sharing a common profession or interests

62. Tyranny: cruel or oppressive government or rule

63. Despotism: the exercise of absolute power; especially in a cruel and oppressive way

64. Monarchy: a form of government with the monarch at the head

65. Aristocracy: the highest class in certain societies, especially those holding hereditary titles or offices; a form of government in which power is held by the nobility

66. Ostentatious: characterized by vulgar or pretentious display; designed to impress or attract notice.

67. Pretentious: attempting to impress by affecting greater importance, talent, culture, etc., than is actually possessed

68. virtuous: having or showing high moral standards.

69. dogmatism: the tendency to lay down principles as incontrovertibly true, without consideration of evidence or the opinions of others

70. fanaticism: The quality of being Fanatical; filled with excessive and single-minded zeal - not accepted.

71. provocateurs: a person who provokes trouble, causes dissension or the like; agitator" - out of fashion, discounted

72. eccentric: of a person or their behavior, unconventional and slightly strange - outcasted

73. vanity: excessive pride in one's own appearance or achievements

74. conspiracist: a person who supports a conspiracy theory; an explanation of an event that it claims was the result of a secret and often complex and evil plot by multiple people

75. Hardliners: a member of a group, typically a political group, who adheres uncompromisingly to a set of ideas or policies

76. legacy: the long-lasting impact of particular events, actions, etc. that took place in the past, or of a person's life

77. toil: work extremely hard or incessantly

78. temperance: abstinence from alcoholic drink; The quality of moderation or self-restraint

79. eloquent: fluent or persuasive in speaking or writing

80. timeless: not affected by the passage of time or changes in fashion

81. anonymous: (of a person) not identified by name; of unknown name

82. Intrepid: fearless, adventurous (often used for humorous effect)

83. Exemplify: be a typical example of

84. ambitions: a strong desire to do or to achieve something, typically requiring determination and hard work

85. customs: the official department that administers and collects the duties levied by a government on imported goods.

86. democracy: a system of government by the whole population or all the eligible members of a state, typically through elected representatives.

87. abolitionists: a person who favors the abolition of a practice or institution.

88. posterity: all future generations of people

89. Moderation: the avoidance of excess or extremes; especially in one's behaviors or political opinions

90. frivolous: not having any serious purpose or value.

91. overbearing: unpleasantly or arrogantly domineering.

92. narcissist: a person who has an excessive interest or admiration in themselves

93. clinical: relating to the observation and treatment of actual patients rather than theoretical or laboratory studies

94. repulsive: arousing intense distaste or disgust.

95. cryotherapy: the use of extreme cold in surgery or other medical treatment

96. Equilibrium: a state of balance or a stable situation where opposing forces cancel each other out and where no changes are occurring

Chapter 5

97. forbearance: patient self-control; restraint and tolerance.

98. counterintuitive: contrary to intuition or to common-sense expectation (but often nevertheless true).

99. perversity: a deliberate desire to behave in an unreasonable or unacceptable way; contrariness

Chapter 6

100. righteous: (of a person or conduct) morally right or justifiable; virtuous

101. crass: lacking sensitivity, refinement, or intelligence.

102. mortal enemy: someone one hates very much and for a long time

103. emblem: a heraldic device or symbolic object as a distinctive badge of a nation, organization, or family.

104. temptation: the desire to do something, especially something wrong or unwise.

105. poverty: the state of being extremely poor.

106. beguiling: charming or enchanting, often in a deceptive way.

107. disorientated: having lost one's sense of direction

108. distorted: giving a misleading or false account or impression; misrepresented.

109. vitriol: cruel and bitter criticism.

110. despot: a ruler or other person who holds absolute power, typically one who exercises it in a cruel or oppressive way

111. tyrant: a cruel and oppressive ruler

112. cognitive bias: a systematic error in thinking that occurs when people are processing and interpreting information

113. bloviate: talk at length, especially in an inflated or empty way

114. sensationalize: present information about (something) in a way that provokes public interest and excitement, at the expense of accuracy.

115. nuance: a subtle difference in or shade of meaning, expression, or sound

116. binary: relating to, composed of, or involving two things

117. delegitimize: withdraw legitimate status or authority from (someone or something

118. Vortex: a mass of whirling fluid or air, especially a whirlpool or whirlwind

119. fallacy: a mistaken belief, especially one based on unsound argument.

120. perpetuate: make (something, typically an undesirable situation or an unfounded belief) continue indefinitely unwittingly: without being aware; unintentionally

121. universal: of, affecting, or done by all people or things in the world or in a particular group; applicable to all cases

Chapter 7

122. reason: the power of the mind to think, understand, and form judgments by a process of logic.

123. cosmopolitanism: the ideology that all human beings belong to a single community, based on a shared morality

124. tenet: a principle or belief, especially one of the main principles of a religion or philosophy

125. Ubuntu: a quality that includes the essential human virtues; compassion and humanity

126. literal: taking words in their usual or most basic sense without metaphor or allegory

127. figurative: departing from a literal use of words; metaphorical

128. exponentially: (of an increase) becoming more and more rapid

129. uncompromising: showing an unwillingness to make concessions to others, especially by changing one's ways or opinions

130. predestined: (of an outcome or course of events) determined in advance by divine will or fate

131. magnificence: impressively beautiful, elaborate, or extravagant; striking

132. reconcile: restore friendly relations between

133. contemplative: expressing or involving prolonged thought.

134. immeasurable: too large, extensive, or extreme to measure

135. prophetic: accurately describing or predicting what will happen in the future

136. ultimate: the best achievable or imaginable of its kind

137. disorder: a state of confusion

138. ardent: enthusiastic or passionate

139. figments: a thing that someone believes to be real but that exists only in their imagination

140. indiscretion: behavior or speech that is indiscreet or displays a lack of good judgment

141. speculation: the forming of a theory or conjecture without firm evidence

142. innuendo: an allusive or oblique remark or hint, typically a suggestive or disparaging one

143. conjecture: an opinion or conclusion formed on the basis of incomplete information

144. resounding: unmistakable; emphatic.

145. patriot: a person who vigorously supports their country and is prepared to defend it against enemies or detractors.

Chapter 8

146. Imperialistic: a policy of extending a country's power and influence through diplomacy or military force

147. marginalize: treat (a person, group, or concept) as insignificant or peripheral

148. radical: especially of change or action) relating to or affecting the fundamental nature of something; far-reaching or

thorough

149. stereotype: a widely held but fixed and oversimplified image or idea of a particular type of person or thing.

150. Ideology: a system of ideas and ideals, especially one which forms the basis of economic or political theory and policy.

151. conspire: make secret plans jointly to commit an unlawful or harmful act.

152. Xenophilia: an affection for unknown/foreign objects, manners, culture, and people

153. blasphemy: the act or offense of speaking sacrilegiously about God or sacred things; profane talk

154. xenophobe: a person having a dislike of or prejudice against people from other countries

155. propaganda: information, especially of a biased or misleading nature, used to promote or publicize a particular political cause or point of view.

156. caricature: a picture, description, or imitation of a person in which certain striking characteristics are exaggerated in order to create a comic or grotesque effect

157. plague: a contagious bacterial disease characterized by fever and delirium

Chapter 9

158. hubris: excessive pride or self-confidence

159. comity: courtesy and considerate behavior toward others

160. ad hominem: (of an argument or reaction) directed against a person rather than the position they are maintaining

161. zealot: a person who is fanatical and uncompromising in pursuit of their religious, political, or other ideals.

162. irreconcilable: (of ideas, facts, or statements) representing findings or points of view that are so different from each other that they cannot be made compatible.

163. militia: a military force that is raised from the civil population to supplement a regular army in an emergency

164. imperialism: a policy of extending a country's power and influence through diplomacy or military force

165. bellicose: demonstrating aggression and willingness to fight.

166. apocalyptic: describing or prophesying the complete destruction of the world.

167. enmity: the state or feeling of being actively opposed or hostile to someone or something

168. embolden: give (someone) the courage or confidence to do something or to behave in a certain way

169. demagoguery: political activity or practices that seek support by appealing to the desires and prejudices of ordinary people rather than by using rational argument

170. ubiquitous: present, appearing, or found everywhere.

171. agitators: a person who urges others to protest or rebel.

172. exploit: make full use of and derive benefit from (a resource)

173. adherent: someone who supports a particular party, person, or set of ideas.

174. ethno-nationalist: someone who believes nations are defined by common ancestry, language, and beliefs

175. Great Replacement Theory: a far-right conspiracy theory

alleging that left-leaning domestic or international elites are attempting to replace white citizens with nonwhite (i.e., Black, Hispanic, Asian, or Arab) immigrants.

176. biblical: very great; on a large scale

177. perfect storm: a particularly bad or critical state of affairs, arising from a number of negative and unpredictable factors.

178. opaque: not able to be seen through; not transparent

179. myth: a widely held but false belief or idea

180. gnats: a small two-winged fly that resembles a mosquito. Gnats include both biting and nonbiting forms, and they typically form large swarms

Chapter 10

181. dumbfounded: greatly astonished or amazed

182. intrigue: the idea that the senses provide us with direct awareness of objects as they really are.

183. intrinsic: belonging naturally; essential

184. awestruck: filled with or revealing awe

185. immunize: make (a person or animal) resistant to a particular infectious disease or pathogen, typically by vaccination

186. Herd mentality: the tendency for people's behavior or beliefs to conform to those of the group to which they belong

187. Polio: an infectious disease especially of young children that is caused by the poliovirus

188. The Bubonic Plague: plague caused by a bacterium (Yersinia pestis) and characterized especially by the formation of

buboes; Called the Black Death, it killed millions of Europeans during the Middle Ages

189. Covid: Coronavirus disease (COVID-19) is an infectious disease caused by the SARS-CoV-2 virus

190. insurrection: a violent uprising against an authority or government.

Chapter 11

191. dog whistle: a subtly aimed political message which is intended for, and can only be understood by, a particular group

192. casualty: a person killed or injured in a war or accident.

193. pestilence: a fatal epidemic disease, especially bubonic plague

194. infiltrate: enter or gain access to (an organization, place, etc.) surreptitiously and gradually, especially in order to acquire secret information

195. emulate: match or surpass (a person or achievement), typically by imitation.

196. slander: make false and damaging statements about (someone)

197. rationalize: attempt to explain or justify (one's own or another's behavior or attitude) with logical, plausible reasons, even if these are not true or appropriate

198. Elitist: a person who believes that a society or system should be led by an elite

199. shambles: a state of total disorder.

200. debunk: expose the falseness or hollowness of (a myth, idea, or belief)

201. censorship: the suppression or prohibition of any parts of books, films, news, etc. that are considered obscene, politically unacceptable, or a threat to security.

202. uninspired: lacking in imagination or originality.

203. welfare: financial support given to people in need.

204. brawn: physical strength in contrast to intelligence

205. credible: able to be believed; convincing.

206. strategic: relating to the identification of long-term or overall aims and interests and the means of achieving them

207. tactical: relating to or constituting actions carefully planned to gain a specific military end

208. commingle: mix, blend

209: confute: prove (a person or an assertion) to be wrong.

Chapter 12

212. patriotism: the quality of being patriotic; devotion to and vigorous support for one's country

213. Osama bin Laden: also known as Usama bin Laden—was a violent terrorist and mass murderer who used bombings and bloodshed to advance his extremist goals

214. Patriots' Day: the anniversary of the battles of Lexington and Concord (1775), celebrated the third Monday in April: a legal holiday in Massachusetts and Maine

215. bipartisan: involving the agreement or cooperation of two political parties that usually oppose each other's policies

216. legislation: laws, considered collectively

217. profusely: to a great degree; in large amounts

218. lament: a passionate expression of grief or sorrow

219. discriminate: having or showing refined taste or good judgment; make an unjust or prejudicial distinction in the treatment of different categories of people, especially on the grounds of ethnicity, sex, age or disability

Chapter 14

220. replete: filled or well-supplied with something

221. Emancipation Proclamation: the proclamation issued by President Lincoln on September 22, 1862, that freed the people held as slaves in those territories still in rebellion against the Union from January 1, 1863, forward.

Chapter 15

222. impeccably: in accordance with the highest standards; faultlessly

223. symmetrical: made up of exactly similar parts facing each other or around an axis; showing symmetry

224. astonishing: extremely surprising or impressive; amazing

225. wallow: roll about or lie relaxed in mud or water

226. condemned: sentenced to a particular punishment, especially death

227. ordered liberty: freedom limited by the need for order in society

Bibliography

Amen, D. (2008). *Change Your Brain, Change Your Life.* Harmony.

Ansart, G. (2015). *Condorcet.* Penn State Press.

Blankenhorn, D. B. (2019). Can Humility Save Us? : Ten Ways to Defuse Political Arrogance. *The American Interest*

Bradford, J., & Townsend, A. (1842). *The writings of John Bradford.*

Brooks, D. (2015). *The Road to Character.* Random House.

Brooks, D. (2012). *The Social Animal: The Hidden Sources of Love, Character, and Achievement.* Random House Trade Paperbacks.

Carnegie, D. (2022). *How To Win Friends And Influence People.* DigiCat.

CBS News. (2022, November 7). What prepping looks like in 2022: Stocking up and skilling up for extreme catastrophes | 60 Minutes. *CBS News.*

Cole, B., Carnegie, D., & Associates, D. C. &. (2012). *How to win friends and influence people in the digital age.* Simon and Schuster.

Cornell, S. C. (2006). What Does Postmodern Mean? *Summit Ministries.*

Damon, W. (2008). *Moral Child: Nurturing Children's Natural Moral Growth.* Simon and Schuster.

Davidson, R. J. (2012). *The Emotional Life of Your Brain.* Penguin.

Dehaene, S. D. (2020). *Time: The Science of Learning: The Secret Brainpower   of Babies* [Google Books]. Meredith Corporation.

Dweck, C. S. (2013). *Self-theories*. Psychology Press.

Eleanor Roosevelt Papers: Speech Before Women's Division Of The United   Jewish Appeal Of Greater New York. (in press). *Encyclopedia.com, 1*.

Greenblatt, J. (2022). *It could happen here: Why America Is Tipping from Hate   to the Unthinkable—And How We Can Stop It*. HarperCollins.

Goggins, D. (2021). *Can't Hurt Me: Master Your Mind and Defy the Odds.*   David Goggins.

Gomes, P. J. (2009). *The Good Life: Truths That Last in Times of Need*. Harper

Collins.Haidt, J. (2006). *The Happiness Hypothesis*. Basic Books

Haidt, J. (2013). *The Righteous Mind: Why Good People Are Divided by   Politics and Religion*. Vintage.

Haidt, J. (2022, December 29). Why the Past 10 Years of American Life Have   Been Uniquely Stupid. *The Atlantic*.

Haidt, J., & Lukianoff, G. (2018). *The Coddling of the American Mind: How   Good Intentions and Bad Ideas Are Setting Up a Generation for   Failure.*

Hanson, M. (2023, January 1). *Alcohol Abuse Statistics [2023]: National +   State Data- NCDAS*. NCDAS.

Incarceration rates by country 2023. (n.d.). https://worldpopulationreview.com/country-rankings/ incarcerati on- rates-by-country

Jacoby, J. (2022, June 7). I'm right, and you're an evil monster. *BostonGlobe.com*. Jenkins, B. M. (2021, November 14).

Kight, S. K. (2023, February 26). *Tens of thousands of Americans have welcomed Ukrainian refugees.* axios.com.

Kushner, H. S. (2011). *Living a Life that Matters: Resolving the Conflict Between Conscience and Success.* Pan Macmillan.

Jerome, R. J. (2021). *The Power of Learning: Building Blocks of Knowledge: All We Do is Learn.* Meredith Premium. (p.4)

Lifeskills South Florida. (2023, March 15). *Anxiety Disorders Treatment | Florida | Lifeskills South Florida.*

Major Depression. (n.d.). National Institute of Mental Health (NIMH). https://www.nimh.nih.gov/health/statistics/major-depression

Magee, B. (2016). *The story of Philosophy.*

Mazzarelli, A. J., & Trzeciak, S. (2019). *Compassionomics: The Revolutionary Scientific Evidence that Caring Makes a Difference.*

Merrit, K. L. M. (2016). Race, Reconstruction, and Reparations. *AAIHS - African American Intellectual History Society.* https://www.aaihs.org/race-reconstruction/

Metaxas, E. (2016). *If you can keep it: The Forgotten Promise of American Liberty.* Penguin.

Mischel, W. (2014). The Marshmallow Test: Understanding Self-control and How To Master It.

Morris, T. (2023). *The Everyday Patriot: How to Be a Great American Now.*

Moss, E. M., McIntosh, K. M., Edelberg, W. E., Broady, K. B., & The Brookings Institution. (2020, December 8). *The*

Black-white wealth gap left Black households more vulnerable. brookings.edu.

Plato, & Fowler, H. N. (1947). *Plato, with an English Translation*.

Podcasts. (2019, September 25). Brandon Novak. https:// brandonnovak.com/podcasts/

Quinn, D. (2020, December 28). What are Dantian? the energy centers of   Chinese medicine. Healthline.

Ritchie, L. C. (2021, December 7). The U.S. surgeon general issues a stark   warning about the state of youth mental health. NPR.

Robertson, D. J. (2019). *How to think like a Roman emperor: The Stoic   Philosophy of Marcus Aurelius*. St. Martin's Press.

Rutherford, N. (2022b, February 24). Why our pursuit of happiness may be   flawed. *BBC Future*.

Sacks, J. (2020). *Morality: Restoring the Common Good in Divided Times*. Hachette UK.

Shapiro, F. R., & Epstein, J. (2006). The Yale book of quotations. In *Yale   University Press eBooks*. http:// ci.nii.ac.jp/ncid/BA79266173

Skousen, W. C. (1981). *The Five Thousand Year Leap*. Verity Publishing.

Sparks, D. (2020). Narcissistic personality disorder: Inflated sense of   importance. *Mayo Clinic News Netwo*

TEDx Talks. (2016, December 20). Help make America talk again | Celeste Headlee | TEDxSeattle [Video]. YouTube.

Pape, R. P. (2023, January 30). *JANUARY 2023 SURVEY REPORT: New Insight into Support for Political Violence From the Right and Left*.   UChicago

CPost.

Roosevelt, T. R. (n.d.). *The Man with the Muck-rake.* americanrhetoric.com.

US Department of Health and Human Services [HHS] (Ed.). (2022). HHS Announces Nearly $35 Million To Strengthen Mental Health Support for Children and Young Adults. *SAMHSA.*

Winfrey, O. (n.d.). *Goodreads | Meet your next favorite book.* Goodreads; Goodreads. Retrieved June 21, 2023, from http://goodreads.com

Yinyang (Yin-yang) | Internet Encyclopedia of Philosophy. (n.d.). https://iep.utm.edu/yinyang/

About the Author

A concerned father who, in 2021, sat down to write a simple birthday card to his son and found himself uniquely incap able of finding the right words. A part-time teacher who shared with his remarkable young students an overwhelming fear of what our society was becoming and was at a complete loss to explain the confusion. A businessman who realizes he had carelessly become just another onlooker to the mess. A truth seeker who goes on his own journey to find some central grounding authority. A humble human who, after years of research and experience, has come to know that it actually exists. Letters to Mikey is the author's first and last book because he cannot imagine that he has anything more important to say. His research, resources, and a concrete plan of action for positive change can be found at www.gettingalong.com.

Made in the USA
Middletown, DE
19 November 2023

43077028R00126